NO CRYSTAL STAIR

NO CRYSTAL STAIR
Womanist Spirituality

Diana L. Hayes

ORBIS BOOKS
Maryknoll, New York 10545

ORBIS BOOKS
Maryknoll, New York 10545

Fathers and Brothers
MARYKNOLL

Founded in 1970, Orbis Books endeavors to publish works that enlighten the mind, nourish the spirit, and challenge the conscience. The publishing arm of the Maryknoll Fathers and Brothers, Orbis seeks to explore the global dimensions of the Christian faith and mission, to invite dialogue with diverse cultures and religious traditions, and to serve the cause of reconciliation and peace. The books published reflect the views of their authors and do not represent the official position of the Maryknoll Society. To learn more about Maryknoll and Orbis Books, please visit our website at www.maryknollsociety.org.

Library of Congress Cataloging-in-Publication Data

Names: Hayes, Diana L., author.
Title: No crystal stair : womanist spirituality / Diana L. Hayes.
Description: Maryknoll : Orbis Books, 2016. | Includes bibliographical references and index.
Identifiers: LCCN 2016001636 | ISBN 9781626981959 (pbk.)
Subjects: LCSH: African American Catholics. | African American women—Religious life. | Spiritual life—Catholic Church. | Womanist theology.
Classification: LCC BX1407.N4 H43 2016 | DDC 248.8/4308996073—dc23
LC record available at http://lccn.loc.gov/2016001636

To my sisters wherever they gather
The strong women keep a'comin'.

ACKNOWLEDGEMENTS

I have been blessed throughout my life by the support and guidance of many who helped to shape and form my understanding of God. That blessing has translated into the work I find myself doing today, seeking to uncover, recover, and present an understanding of spirituality from the perspective of persons of African descent in the United States; spiritualities, for there are certainly more than one, that emerged from their lived experiences both in Africa and in the Americas. Theirs is a story of a constant and sustaining encounter with God that saw them through all afflictions, great and small, and enabled them to rejoice even in the midst of their tears.

I thank the many women in my life, sisters and mothers, who taught me, guided me, comforted me, and helped to prepare the paths I have walked. I thank the many men in my life, also teachers, guides, protectors, who encouraged me on my way.

I thank my many students over the years that poked and prodded, questioned and argued, and helped me to develop a sense of myself as a child of God while they were growing into their own sense of self as well.

Most of all I thank God with whom I became acquainted at a very young age and who has never failed me yet.

Thank you.

Contents

Mother to Son

By Langston Hughes

Well, son, I'll tell you
Life for me ain't been no crystal stair.
It's had tacks in it.
And splinters,
And boards torn up,
And places with no carpet on the floor—
Bare.
But all the time
I'se been a climbin' on, And reachin' landin's,
And turnin' corners,
And sometimes goin' in the dark
Where there ain't been no light.
So, boy, don't you turn back.
Don't you set down on the steps
'Cause you finds it's kinder hard.
Don't you fall now—
For I'se still goin', honey,
I'se still climbin',
And life for me ain't been no crystal stair.

(From *Collected Poems*, 1994)

Introduction

A Womanist Spiritual Journey

"Life for me ain't been no crystal stair."[1] With these words Langston Hughes poignantly sets forth the lived experience of women of African descent in the United States. In the short but eloquent poem from which this line is taken, he lays out the contours and content of African American women's spirituality, a spirituality forged in the fiery furnaces of slavery, Jim Crow, and ongoing prejudice and discrimination in these United States. For over 450 years, black women have struggled, fought, journeyed, and climbed, with their men and sometimes urging them on, carrying their children and giving them a boost when needed, picking up strays along the way, "keepin' on." It was not an easy journey; their path was not laid out for them, swept down, neat and tidy. As Hughes affirms, that path, too often uphill, "had tacks in it, and splinters, and boards torn up, and places with no carpet on the floor—bare."[2] Yet, they kept climbing. Somehow they made it over.

The spirituality of black women in the United States is a womanist spirituality, one that flows from their lived encounters with God, nurtured and sustained with sweat, tears, and, yes, at

---

Parts of this chapter are based on materials found in my *Hagar's Daughters: Womanist Ways of Being in the World* (Mahwah, NJ: Paulist Press, 1995).

times blood, as they worked the fields, worked in the homes of white families, worked in factories and wherever else they could to support their families and build their communities. They did not have the luxury of staying home and caring for their own but had to go out into the world to confront racism and sexism in all its forms.

Theirs is a spirituality grounded in their faith in a God who affirmed their worth as human beings created in God's own image and likeness. In the words of the psalmist, "The Lord is my light and my salvation, whom shall I fear?" (Ps 27:1). This question, in actuality, is more a statement of undying and un-self-conscious faith that can be said to serve as the foundation of African American women's spirituality. It is a spirituality which arises from a deep and abiding faith in a God of love, a wonder-working God who walked and talked with them, giving them the strength to persevere. This God in whom they placed not only their trust but also their very lives as slaves and second-class citizens in the United States for over four hundred years was a God transformed and transforming. Creator of all that existed, God was also a man-child in need of their love, trust, and nurturing. God was a spirit of strength and perseverance that guided them over the rock-strewn paths on which they were forced to travel and a liberating, righteous lover of justice who opposed their oppression and the blasphemy of those who claimed that God was on the oppressor's side. They knew better, for they knew God personally, intimately.

Historically, persons of African descent in the United States have been, in the words of Zora Neale Hurston, a people whose eyes were always watching God.[3] This faith in a God of love and justice gave them the strength to "keep on keepin' on" knowing that "[God's] eye is on the sparrow and I know [God] watches me."[4] Nothing was too hard for God and, as a result, nothing was too hard for them to attempt to accomplish in their everyday struggle to keep hope and love alive.

African American women's spirituality is deeply rooted in a community of the born, yet to be born, and those who have already passed over. This community forms a great cloud of witnesses who help to shape and form all people into the human beings God intended them to be. Throughout history, life outside of the community was inconceivable; life over against the community was suicidal. The community, from smallest child to oldest elder, was the life's blood of each and every individual within it, regardless of age, gender, or ranking, and each one owed a responsibility to others within that community to enable both community and individuals to survive and to thrive.

Faith in God and in their community of shared faith and oppression gave enslaved women hope, enabling them to persevere against daunting obstacles which threatened not simply their identity but their very lives. Somehow they were able to forge a spirituality, a holistic and pervasive understanding of the interconnectedness and interdependence of all of creation with God that has now persisted for centuries. They took to heart the prophetic words of Sojourner Truth: "If the first woman God ever made was strong enough to turn the world upside down all alone, together women ought to be able to turn it right-side up again."[5]

Maria W. Stewart, the first black female political writer in the United States, asked: "How long shall the fair daughters of Africa be compelled to bury their minds and talents beneath a load of iron pots and kettles?"[6] She called on them to come forth in their diversity and claim their lives and those of their men and children as worthy of pride, proclaiming in 1831: "O, Ye daughters of Africa! Awake! Arise! No longer sleep nor slumber, but distinguish yourselves, show forth to the world that ye are endowed with noble and exalted faculties."[7]

Black women have taken up her challenge, working to erase the stereotyped images of black women still prevalent in the United States, of Mammy, Jezebel, Aunt Jemima, and Sapphire, replacing them with the true images of black women as proud, intelligent, hard-working, faith-filled women upon whom the lives of their families and the black community and black churches depend.

I think of my mother, now gone home to be with God, and how she struggled and fought to ensure that her children, four girls, would have opportunities that she had not had. She was one of those women that Alice Walker spoke of:

> *They were women then*
> *My momma's generation*
> *Husky of voice—stout of step*
> *With fists as well as*
> *Hands*
> *How they battered down*
> *Doors*
> *And ironed*
> *Starched white*
> *Shirts*
> *How they led*
> *Armies*
> *Headragged Generals*
> *Across mined*
> *Fields*
> *Booby-trapped kitchens*
> *To discover books*
> *Desks*
> *A place for us*
> *How they knew what we*
> *Must know*
> *Without knowing a page*
> *Of it*
> *Themselves.*[8]

And so our mothers and grandmothers have, more often than not anonymously, handed on the creative spark, the seed of the flower they themselves never hoped to see; or like a sealed letter they could not plainly read. They had the spirit within them, unnamed perhaps but rarely unknown, the spirit which "brought them through" as they sang:

> *Sometimes I feel discouraged*
> *And think my work's in vain*
> *And then the Holy Spirit*
> *Revives my soul again.*
> *There is a balm in Gilead*
> *To make the wounded whole*
> *There is a balm in Gilead*
> *To heal the sin sick soul.*[9]

An anonymous former slave woman put it another way; "I have seen nothing nor heard nothing, but only felt the Spirit in my soul, and I believe that will save me when I come to die."[10]

Where do we look for the source of that "creative spark" in our mothers and grandmothers, who sought to make flowers bloom wherever they found a barren piece of soil, whether of earthen clay or within a child's mind? We, who are now rooted in another soil, look homeward to Africa, our motherland. bell hooks, like so many other creative black women, realizes:

The spiritual world of my growing up was very akin to those described in novels by Toni Morrison, Paule Marshall, or Ntozake Shange. There was in our daily life an ever present and deep engagement with the mystical dimensions of Christian faith. There was the secret love of the ancestors—the Africans and native Americans—who had given that new race of black folk, born here on this portion of earth, whole philosophies about how to be One with the universe and sustain life. That lore was shared by the oldest of the old, the secret believers, the ones who had kept the faith.

In the traditional world of black folk experience, there was (and remains in some places and certainly in many hearts) a profound unspoken belief in the spiritual power of black people to transform our world and live with integrity and oneness despite oppressive social realities. In that world, black folks collectively believed in "higher powers," knew that forces stronger than the will and intellect of humankind shaped and determined our existence, the way we lived.[11]

It was that knowledge, formed within us as part of our African heritage, passed down somehow from parent to child, which provided the fire that forged the strength which enabled us to not simply survive, but to "move on up a little higher" each time. Although not a literate people at first, black people, especially their women, were the "keepers of the faith, the "bearers of culture," and the persistent "fanners of the flame" of that "creative spark" Alice Walker and others have come to recognize within us.

My mother had that "spark" deeply embedded within her even though she was required to leave school at the age of ten in order to work to help support her family of eleven. The only work available to a young black woman in rural Tennessee was domestic: cleaning, washing, and cooking for white families. A black woman's life in the Depression-era South was a difficult one, fraught with the danger of sexual assault, the threat of job loss for not being submissive or for "talking back." It was not an easy life for an adult, let alone a child. Yet she and her sisters persevered. As she told me many years later, she hated every minute of it. But she bided her time, eventually married the boy next door, my father, and moved North to greater freedom, albeit to a life still tainted by prejudice and discrimination.

How did they do it? I have been blessed with several mothers over the course of my life who passed that "spark" on to me and fanned it furiously whenever it threatened to go out. I have watched and listened and learned from all of them what it means to be a woman of African descent in the United States. They, with their steadfast pace, their fervent faith, and their determination to "make it over" enabled me to begin my own journey, one that, as for them and so many of their black sisters, involved a lot of climbing, searching, struggling, and determination. These four women, my mother, Helen Louise Dodson Hayes, my maternal aunt, Mildred Dodson Jackson, my godmother, Ollie Cook, and my other-mother, Lucretia Diggs, saw something in me that initially I was unable to see myself, something that enabled me to become the person I am today. All four are now home with God, but the lessons they taught me with sternness and love sustain me to this day and continue to empower me to speak of the spiritually rich lives of black women, who possess a spirituality that burns deeply within them and is expressed in a multitude of ways. They sought not merely a "room of one's own" in which to write, to be free, to create and be, in turn, re-created; they sought and were too often denied a life of their own, a being, a freedom which was of their own making and owed nothing to the false largesse of a master or a mistress or, sometimes, even of a husband.

How did they do it? How did they manage to keep their creativity alive year after year and century after century when, for most of the years black people have been in the United States, it was a punishable crime for a black person to learn how to read or write? And the freedom to paint, to sculpt, to expand their minds with liberating and creative actions of any kind simply did not exist.[12]

How did they continue to sing, to pray, to sew quilts worthy of hanging in museums throughout this land? How did they do it, and more important, how did they pass it on—to me and to my sisters, those before and those coming after me. My journey, like theirs, has been one of ups and downs, of forward progress and backwards retreat, of moments of clarifying epiphanies and others of deep doubt and despair. Yet, like many of my mothers before me, I drew upon my faith in a wonder-working God, a God of possibility and opportunity, a God who loved me into life and, despite all, continues to sustain and guide me to the present day. My faith was formed in the African Methodist Episcopal Zion Church, a historically black Protestant denomination. There I learned of God's love for me as it was lived out by church members who guided, counseled, and loved me without question.

St. Luke's, like most black churches of the 1950s and 1960s, was a refuge for its members, a source of spirituality but also of learning and freedom. Our lives revolved around the feast days and holy days, the celebration of birthdays, weddings, funerals, baptisms, graduations, and other milestones in our lives. It was a resource for our growing political engagement with the world around us. All of my earliest memories are of growing up in that church: Sunday school, Girl Scouts, Vacation Bible School, picnics, parties, even movies. The church was truly the center of our lives. My father was the Pastor's Steward and my mother was in the Senior Choir, the Ideal Club (the women's club), and many other organizations within the church. It was at St. Luke's that my faith was shaped and formed and my understanding of God and my relationship with God developed.

From my earliest years, I have felt a closeness to God that manifested itself strangely enough—for a young black woman growing up in an urban environment—in nature. Throughout my life I have felt an awareness of God, especially when I have found myself in the woods or mountains, that I have not quite understod. I remember rejoicing when we would go on picnics or to parks. I would wander off and place myself in a stillness and peace that I did not fully understand but that helped me to withstand the trials and tribulations of my young life. I spoke to God in those brief interludes and I believe that God responded, not so much in words, but in a deep sense of contentment and love.

I escaped outdoors whenever I could and loved it when my Girl Scout troop went to Seven Hills Camp for several days in the summer. To my dismay, I discovered that I was the only one that truly enjoyed those days and nights spent in the woods. My sister Scouts hated them. This was when I began to truly realize that I was, indeed, "different," as my sisters and others had often told me. I liked the outdoors. I liked to read, anything and everything I could get my hands on. I loved to study (though I found actual school somewhat boring); I was a "tomboy," and my best friends were the boys in the neighborhood. I loved learning languages. I knew by the time I was in sixth grade that I was going to college. I also knew I would never marry. When I was ten, I gave my life to God in return for God's promise to enable me to care for my mother and sisters. I did this because, initially, I wanted to defend them from my father's aggression. He was a wonderful father until he drank, at which time he turned into a monster who was physically abusive, especially toward my mother and older sister. I saw myself as their defender and, in many ways, I still do.

Turning my life over to God was incredibly freeing in many ways. I believed that God would call on me at some point, but in the meantime I was able to learn, grow, and explore in so many ways. I fell in love with classical music and became involved in singing in choirs and playing the French horn at my high school. Those four years, marred only by my father's outbursts, were wonderful as I grew in self-confidence and knowledge of myself.

When I was sixteen, however, I stopped going to St. Luke's or any church, feeling that there was too much hypocrisy in the institutional church. Quoting from e. e. cummings' poem, "i am a little church (no great cathedral),"[13] I told my parents that I felt closer to God in the woods than sitting on a pew in church. Fortunately, my mother convinced my dad to let me stop going. As she put it: "She didn't say she no longer believes in God," and she was correct. It was just that my God was not to be found in buildings or institutions but outdoors. I did not become affiliated with a church again until I was thirty-two, when I became, much to my surprise, a Roman Catholic.

Throughout college and law school, I spent as much time outdoors as I could. While at law school in the early 1970s, I became a part of the youth hostel movement and was finally able to fully indulge in life in the outdoors. I canoed and kayaked, skied and swam, hiked and climbed mountains, all of the things I had dreamed of doing all of my life. Then in 1975 I injured my knees, an injury that put an end to my outdoor life and has haunted me ever since. This caused a serious spiritual crisis for me as I tried to understand God's actions. Why would he take away that which I loved most? It was then, after I had moved to Albany, New York, to work as an attorney that God came to me and called me out of my old world into a new one I had not at all foreseen. It was then that I began to realize that all that had gone before was simply preparation for this new and challenging but fulfilling life into which God was calling me.

God's call was explicit but also confusing and came in two parts. "I want you to look into the Catholic Church" was the first request, repeated over and over during the summer and fall of 1979 till it filled my every waking and sleeping moment. Finally, after much resistance—because it made absolutely no sense to me, having had no prior experience of the Catholic Church—I did look into the Catholic Church and with the guidance of Fr. Nellis Tremblay became a Catholic in December of 1979. Doing so satisfied the deep longing I had been experiencing which had made me dissatisfied with all aspects of my life until I became a Catholic. I had become a lawyer after working on Robert Kennedy's 1968 presidential campaign. Having majored in urban and poverty law, I hoped to be able to help those less fortunate than I. Instead I found myself doing legislative work which, for the most part, I felt helped no one and bored me to tears.

By 1979, I had decided to enter the U.S. Foreign Service, which I felt would fit with my love of learning languages and satisfy my longing to travel. I had passed all of the exams and been invited to enter the January 1980 class but had to postpone my entrance when my legs failed me to the point that I was bedridden for several weeks in the fall of 1979 and the spring of 1980. It was during this time that I received God's second request. It was phrased more demandingly: "You will go to Catholic University and study theology." What? I had no idea where or even what Catholic University was and what it meant to study theology or actually what theology was, but after much inner struggle and too many "coincidences" that Fr. Tremblay saw as God's action in my life, I finally agreed.

In the fall of 1980 I found myself, on crutches and with both legs in braces, at Catholic University. When I arrived and began my studies, my mind and heart were finally in sync as I found myself able to combine what I was learning about Christianity and myself with what I had learned as an attorney. I was quite surprised to discover that I was the first laywoman to have been accepted into the pontifical doctorate program, which required a minimum of seven years of study. I had applied for it because it seemed the best program for an in-depth course in Catholicism for a brand new convert.

Despite the suspicions of my male classmates, who thought I was either a radical feminist or looking for a husband, I felt finally fulfilled as a vowed celibate laywoman. I had found my appointed role in life, to serve God, the black community, and the church as a theologian. As I learned more about the church's social justice teachings and tradition, I found a strong connection between law and theology that inspired and challenged me. I realized I could use my legal background in conjunction with my growing knowledge of theology to help make a positive difference, I hoped, in the lives of the least among us.

From 1983 to 1985, I worked part time for the archdiocese of Washington as its legislative consultant, and for the first time in my life felt I was where I was meant to be and was truly doing God's will. I was introduced to liberation theologies and began to look for materials on, by, and about persons of African descent in Christianity. Reading the work of newly emerging black theologians set me on course to become a black theologian myself, concerned about, researching, and writing on the black presence in Christianity, especially in the Catholic Church where so many were ignorant of the long history of Africans' engagement with the Christian faith.

I completed the baccalaureate and licentiate in theology at Catholic University (DC) and then went to Leuven (Louvain), Belgium at the recommendation of my mentor, Bishop Howard Hubbard of Albany, New York, whom I had met in the spring of 1980 just before moving to Washington and beginning my studies. There I earned a pontifical doctorate in sacred theology and a PhD in religious studies at the Universiteit Katoliek te Leuven (Louvain) in June of 1988. That fall, I began my professional theological career at Georgetown University.

Looking back over my life and my journey with God, I can more clearly now see where and how God intervened and guided me onto the path I now walk as a Roman Catholic womanist theologian. As I stated earlier, I love to read and had read pretty much all of the books in our branch library—certainly all those in the children's and young adult sections—by the time I graduated from eighth grade. I studied Latin in high school and that enabled me to have the Latin requirement waived at Catholic University. College was everything I had hoped for; I was no longer bored. My initial dream was to be a chemist, but I quickly discovered my preparation was inadequate in comparison with that of my classmates from other schools. I switched to my second love, languages, and majored in French and German, until my senior year when, as I noted above, I was deeply influenced by Robert Kennedy's presidential campaign and switched to political science and pre-law. All of this seeming wandering meant, however, that I was quite prepared for theological studies, as I had the necessary languages and had taken a number of philosophy courses for fun. These things shaped me in myriad ways, but it was not until I began my theological studies that I came to a greater awareness of who I was as an African-descended woman and how that affected me in every aspect of my life.

My spirituality, a womanist spirituality, that is, a spirituality forged in the awareness and experience of the multiplicative forms of oppression that are used to limit and restrain black women, has been honed and sharpened by my journey with God throughout my life. I was always aware of God's presence and trusted that whatever I tried to do, God's grace and mercy would see me through. My studies prepared me for a pivotal encounter in 1984 with Alice Walker's writings, especially her work, *In Search of Our Mother's Gardens: Womanist Prose*,[14] which opened new worlds of possibility and meaning for me as a womanist theologian. I was transformed, as so many other black women in seminaries and theologates were. It was our "aha" moment. I had accepted God's call to become, first a Catholic and second, a Catholic theologian, but I truly had no clear understanding of what these demands entailed. I set forth in faith, believing that God would guide me and help me to understand what I was being called to do.

Throughout my journey, I put my trust in God and those he sent to guide me like my mothers, as well as Fr. Tremblay, who guided my entry into the church, Fr. Carl Peter, who served as my advisor at CUA and introduced me to the work and then the person of James H. Cone, Bishop Howard Hubbard, who continues to guide and mentor me to the present day, and Catholic priests, sisters, brothers, and laypeople from every ethnicity, as well as many others who befriended and supported me on my journey.

At the beginning, I had no idea where I was going, what I would be doing, or even how I would sustain myself. At each turn, God met me and affirmed again and again that he would never leave me. Every step of the way was unclear, but again I put my faith in God and he brought me through. Truly, nothing is too hard for God! God's support was very important to me because I was terrified of public speaking and even as an attorney had found it very difficult to speak up in front of others. The last thing I ever wanted to be was a teacher. So, of course, I realized that was what I was being trained to be. After eight years of intensive theological study in Washington and Belgium, I was hired as an assistant professor at Georgetown University. I still remember the utter shock of the students in my first class as they let out a gasp that echoed throughout the classroom at seeing their first black female theology professor!

It was my deep and abiding faith in a God who answers prayer, a God who works wonders, a God who calls you out into a new reality that sustained and nurtured me. That faith was the faith of my mothers, those four wonderful women who took me under their wing and helped me to trust in myself and in God. Their spirituality is the spirituality of generations of African-descended women who continued to climb those harsh, broken, and splintered stairs regardless of the pain and hardship they experienced while doing so. They neither gave up nor gave in, and they counseled those coming after them to do the same: "all the time I'se been a-climbin' on . . . so don't you turn back. Don't you set down on the steps 'cause you find it kinder hard . . . I'se still climbin' and life for me ain't been no crystal stair."[15]

When I researched and wrote my first monograph, *Hagar's Daughters,* I immersed myself in the lives and voices of black women who had paved the path I was now walking with God's help. They were women like Maria Stewart, Sojourner Truth, Harriet Tubman, Ida B. Wells-Barnett, Mary Terrell, Mary Elizabeth Lange, Henriette de Lille, Anna Julia Cooper, Dorothy Height, Rosa Parks, Ella Baker, Fannie Lou Hamer, Maya Angelou, and so many others known and unknown who refused to allow others to put limitations on their voices or their very being. And so today we, womanist scholars, continue to speak out of our own contexts, from within our own lived experiences, confronting the challenges and silence that have kept us chained and bound to definitions of womanhood not of our own making.

Ours is a God, like Maria Stewart's, who directly intervenes in human affairs, "in the affairs of nations and individuals, against the wicked and on behalf of the downtrodden, but according to [God's] own timetable."[16] We are called to speak out as women by God as she herself was:

> The spirit of God come before me and I spoke before many . . . reflecting on what I had said, I felt ashamed . . . A something said within my breast, "press forward, I will be with thee." And my heart made this reply, "Lord, if thou will be with me, then I will speak for thee as long as I live.[17]

These women speak to me because I too have heard that "something within" that called me out of myself and into a world of possibility. Their lives in so many ways seemed to parallel my own. Their voices were voices I was familiar with from my mothers and other faith-filled women who mentored me through the years. My spirituality was nurtured and sustained by the strong, daring, vocal black women whom I encountered on my journey to God, a journey that continues to this day. They embody what it means to be womanist and to have a womanist spirituality.

What is womanist spirituality? It is the low-voiced croon of a mother to her sleepy child; it is the anguished moan of a woman grieving the senseless loss of a loved one; it is the joy-filled cry of a woman in the pews as she hears the voice of God speaking to her; it is the myriad voices of African-descended women calling out in love, desperation, hope, fear, pain, grief, and joy to a God who knows them, loves them, understands them. Womanist spirituality is the encounter of black women and Jesus spelled out in song, poetry, novels, and memoirs that speak of the everlasting struggle as they continue to move themselves and their people one step closer to the Promised Land, a land to be found after death, yes, but more important, a land they know has been promised in this life as well. Theirs is a struggle, as Delores Williams affirms, not solely for liberation from oppression of whatever kind but for survival and a decent quality of life. To be free is desirable and important, but one has to be prepared for freedom by having the wherewithal to survive and help others to survive. Survival cannot be simply bare endurance. It must be a survival of grace and mercy, one that helps a people to grow and thrive so that when freedom does come, they are prepared to live.[18]

Womanist spirituality is lived and experienced in the every-dayness of life, in the raising of children, your own or others. It is in the haunting memory of loved ones lost to senseless violence at the hands of others. It is in the realization of being seen as "less than" simply because of your skin color or your hairstyle or how you speak. But it is also in the triumphant whoop of a female preacher calling her flock to pay attention now. It is in the steadfastness and stability of the Mothers of the Church watching over those coming along behind them and engaging them in theological dialogue: "You yet holdin' on?" "Yes, ma'am, I'm yet holdin' on." "Then you keep keepin' on, baby," an assurance that they are loved and cared for. Womanist spirituality is a word, a phrase, a movement, an action, all rooted in 450-plus years of black existence in the United States. It is the refiner's gold as witnessed to by countless women tried and tested in the fire and coming forth like pure gold.[19]

As a womanist, I believe that no one is truly free until all are free, whether black or white, rich or poor, straight or LGBTQ. The social constructions that humanity has created, especially Western society, must be pulled down and destroyed using new tools for, as Audre Lorde proclaimed, "the master's tools cannot dismantle the master's house."[20]

This cannot be done alone but only in solidarity with all who seek a better world. As a Catholic womanist theologian, I ground my faith in the social justice teachings of my church, teachings which, sadly, have and continue to be too often overlooked or ignored. These teachings, which affirm the dignity of all of humanity and our relatedness to each other and the world around us, can serve as a resource with which to develop a Catholic womanist theology that is life affirming and community building. As Emilie Townes affirms: "Womanist spirituality is the working out of what it means for each of us to seek compassion, justice, worship, and devotion in our witness. This understanding of spirituality seeks to grow into wholeness of spirit and body, mind and heart—into holiness in God."[21]

This work is a compilation of writings on and about spirituality that I have drafted from my perspective as a womanist over the past twenty-five years. I hope they will reveal the path of my spiritual journeying with God and those around me. I have grown in that time in my understanding of God's action in my life and in the lives of persons of African descent, how we have in our centuries-long sojourn in this country been guided and graced, watched over and blessed by God. I am a Catholic womanist, standing firmly in the shoes my mothers' made for me and walking toward a future in which all of God's creation will be recognized and affirmed regardless of race, class, gender, or sexual orientation. I am black. I am Catholic. And by the grace of God, I am here. I invite you to share my journey of self-discovery and faith, and I hope this work will also serve as a source of inspiration and confirmation for you.

The chapters are as follows:

Chapter 1—"To Be Black, Catholic, and Female": In 1991, I was asked by the staff of the *New Theology Review* to reflect on what it meant to me to be black, female, and Catholic. At this time, there were only a handful of Catholic scholars of African descent in the United States and, like me, they were just starting their academic careers. Ours was a voice new to academia and to the Catholic Church, although earlier black scholars, such as Frs. Bede Abrams, Joseph Nearon, Cyprian Davis, and Edward Braxton, as well as Sr. Thea Bowman had made significant contributions.

The article was to appear in an issue devoted to Catholic scholars from different racial and ethnic origins. When I submitted my article, there was some concern from colleagues who felt I should have written a piece that was more scholarly than the one I wrote, which was somewhat subjective and personal. Their comments made me come to the realization that my desire in writing theology is not to produce dense and incomprehensible pieces crammed with footnotes that the average person in the pew would be unable to comprehend. No, my goal is to break open not just God's word but God's action in human lives. What is God saying to us now? Where is God leading us? How do we, especially as persons of African descent, articulate our faith and spirituality in ways that are reflective of our heritage as deeply religious people?

Thus, I see my audience as those with an interest in learning more about God and their relationship to God in their ordinary daily lives. Writing in this way has caused problems, especially during the tenure process when I was told my writing was too pastoral and not scholarly enough. Yet I felt I had to persevere, and as I became more involved with other womanist theologians I realized that I was not alone. I write from the experience of African-descended women in the African diaspora because their stories, their lives, have yet to be told and need to be told. As I immerse myself in the literature produced by persons of African descent globally, their poetry, essays, memoirs, and other writings, I am able to then build on the spiritual and theological framework they provide me, a framework, a structure that guides and supports all that I do. This article was the beginning of a journey that continues to this day.

Chapter 2—"Slain in the Spirit": This article was written around the same time as the article in chapter 1. In it, I sought to develop an understanding of the Holy Spirit and the role she played and continues to play in the lives of those brought unwillingly to this country and enslaved, and in the lives of their descendants. I had earlier published my first monograph, *Trouble Don't Last Always: Soul Prayers*[22] as I grappled with the severe rheumatoid arthritis that had struck me down in in 1987. In chronicling my struggles and frustrations, I relied on gospel music and spirituals to ease the pain and allow me to relax and rest. I realized that these songs were at the very heart not only of my own self-understanding as a person of faith but of the faith of most persons of African descent in the United States, certainly those who were Christian.

I wanted to understand and share that self-understanding with others by looking at the journey of blacks from Africa to the Americas, recognizing and affirming the critical role that the Holy Spirit played in our ability to persevere in this harsh and oppressive land. (I have since expanded this article and incorporated it into a later work on African American spirituality, *Forged in the Fiery Furnace.*[23])

Chapter 3—"Deep River": In the fall of 1992 I was asked to participate in a day of recollection for faculty and staff at Georgetown University. As I wondered what I could possibly present to a group that was so different from me—the sole African American in the Department of Theology and one of a handful of blacks on campus—the book *Deep River*[24] by black theologian Howard Thurman came to mind, along with the spiritual of the same name. Looking back over my life, with the words of the song playing constantly in the back of my mind, I realized that life in and of itself is a river that ebbs and flows, twists and turns, surprising us along the way. As a person who has loved and spent as much time as possible in nature, I thought of the joys of floating down a river and the sudden rush of rapids followed by the calm of flat water as a metaphor for life as we seek to discern how we are being called and what we are being called to. In the process of living our lives we find there are moments of excitement and action as well as moments of calm and almost boredom. Our paths flow through life and eventually our lives come into contact with the lives of others and are blended or else they flow together for a while and then separate, but eventually, as with the rivers, our lives flow into one, the being of God.

Chapter 4—"Trouble Don't Last Always": My first years of teaching were extremely difficult as I was learning how to present my thoughts and knowledge to my students in ways that challenged and hopefully excited them. As I mentioned earlier, teaching was the last thing I had ever wanted to do because I had a crippling fear of public speaking. Yet here I was in front of a classroom of students astounded at my presence and existence because none of them had ever encountered a black female Catholic theologian (or a male one either) before. The difficulty was exacerbated by the pain and exhaustion of my struggle with rheumatoid arthritis that had left me suffering through sleepless nights and coping with limited mobility. Writing was difficult and painful, and typing was almost impossible; walking and standing were becoming increasingly difficult. I was at my wits' end as to what I could do other than pray for relief. Over the passage of about two weeks, however, I realized that when I awoke in the night, there would be the memory of a song, gospel or spiritual, or a black poem that I remembered. As I lay there with the words and/or melody going through my mind, I felt other words forming and slowly began to write them down. The result was the monograph *Trouble Don't Last Always* in which I poured out my anger, frustrations, fear, doubts, hopes, and aspirations. This chapter is just a sampling of the book, showing some of my progression from anger and fear to acceptance and hope. The result was a lifting of my spirits and, to my surprise, an alleviation of much of the pain as I began to accept my illness and work with rather than fight against it. I had no intention of publishing the monograph until a friend lent it to a young man she knew with multiple sclerosis who prayed with it and was comforted.

Chapter 5—"Were You There?": My mother passed away in April 1998 after a brief illness. Her death was unexpected and came as a terrible shock to me and to my three sisters. She had lived with me during the last ten years of her life and had accompanied me on my travels to give talks all over the United States. The shock of her death sent me on a devastatingly downward spiral, although few knew about it. I look back at the time from April of 1998 through the end of 2000 and have very little memory of anything except her death and my grief.

Some time before that, I had been asked to write a meditation on a series of pictures that depicted the Stations of the Cross on the whitewashed walls of a small church in a village in Tanzania. The artist, Charles Ndege, a young Tanzanian, had brought the passion of Christ to bold and vibrant life. What was most striking was that the passion was presented as taking place in a small African village and all of the people were clearly and beautifully depicted as African. I had had the pictures for some time and would occasionally pull them out and look at them, especially when I was feeling low. One day, as I again sat listening to gospel music and spirituals, words began to form in my mind and I scrambled to write them down, Again, writing the book brought healing to my soul. Some few have challenged the depiction of Christ as black, thus revealing their own ignorance and limited faith, but for many, this book, especially its pictures, has provided spiritual release and healing.

Chapter 6—"Who Do You God Say That We Are?": I was asked to contribute to a collection of essays in honor of Sr. Joan Chittister by writing about what I believed or saw to be a critical spiritual issue for the twenty-first century. In thinking about my response, I realized that a question that had often challenged me was: How does God see us, his creation? Are we living up to God's expectations or have we and do we continue to fail? The answer is, of course, both/and. There are those who have lived and continue to live lives that are exemplary in their honesty, their compassion, their selfless love for others. Then there are the rest of us, fallible human beings trying to walk God's path but too often straying, falling down, running off even to pursue other goals that seem more important. Jesus asked the apostles, "Who do you say that I am?" Is it not time for us to ask God, "Who do you say that I am?" We need to be reminded of the purpose of our creation and of the gift of life that was given us by God. We are called by God to care for, not to dominate, the world and those within it.

Chapter 7—"We Too Are America": On August 29, 2005, one of the greatest catastrophes in American history evolved as Hurricane Katrina, a Category 5 hurricane, devastated the city of New Orleans and the surrounding areas. The impact was horrific, but the true horror was not revealed until after the storm subsided and we saw the images of thousands of New Orleanians stranded on the rooftops of flooded houses and apartment buildings, abandoned in hospitals and on highways, left to fend for themselves in the Superdome and the Convention Center.

Women and children were the worst hit, yet they were also in some vicious paradox blamed for their situation. Even though their city, state, and nation had abandoned them, they somehow managed to persevere. I wrote of the racism and classism that had allowed for such terrible conditions to unfold, showing the lack of preparation or even thought on the part of the various governmental entities, from the federal government to the smallest parish, for those who were the least prepared or able to withstand such a catastrophe. Once again, black women had to draw upon their faith in a God of wonder, a God of righteousness, and, holding their children close and hand in hand with others in the same situation, fight for their lives in order to survive.

Chapter 8—"Woman Offered #5": The artwork of Janet Mackenzie has inspired millions around the world ever since her "Jesus 2000" was unveiled. I had always wanted to reflect and write on her work, but had never had the opportunity until I was invited by editor Sue Perry of Orbis Books to be part of a book dedicated to her work. The picture I was given was *Woman Offered #5*, which depicted a woman hanging on the cross. I immediately thought of how women, especially women of color, had lived lives of surrogacy, both voluntarily and involuntarily, for centuries throughout the world.

As a womanist, I recognize and honor the sacrifice of women who have toiled long and hard in order to care for their families, children, and husbands, and yet still sought a space of their own, as Alice Walker noted, to be creative. It is time, I realized, for women to come down off the crosses that our world and churches have nailed them to and create lives for themselves, lives that provide them with dignity and honor as they continue, and as they always will, to build families and communities where all can not only survive but thrive.

Chapter 9—"Faith of Our Mothers": This talk was given at a historic gathering at Notre Dame University entitled "Uncommon Faithfulness: The Witness of African American Catholics." Members of the black Catholic community at every level of the church came to witness to the centuries-long faith of persons of African descent in the Catholic Church in the United States. Theologians, ethicists, pastoral ministers, priests, deacons, laity, all gathered to testify to and proclaim a faith that had helped them through many difficulties as well as triumphs, despite the institutional church's lukewarm reception and recognition of their deep, long, and abiding presence.

My presentation dealt with African American women and their centuries-long struggle to provide homes, educate children, and build communities of faith despite the resistance and indifference they too often met from those in the hierarchy as well as their own fellow Catholics of different ethnicities. By their persistent and uncommon faithfulness, they model a spirituality of resistance and survival that has withstood the test of time.

Chapter 10—"Insistent Inclusion: Intersections of Race, Class, and Gender": As a part of Catholic women's efforts to propose strategies for reform of the church in the twenty-first century, I was asked to write on womanist ascetical practices. Those of us writing in this area sought to reclaim the historical understanding of Christian asceticism not as individual penitential practices that are all too often body-disparaging but as a comprehensive spiritual practice "that is intentional, regular, and embarked upon in order to cultivate greater authenticity and integration."[25] As a womanist, I call attention in this chapter to the insistent and persistent efforts of all women but especially women of color, women of African descent, who have sought inclusion into the life of the Catholic Church at every level. A church without women is impossible; it is time to utilize the graces and talents of women if the Catholic Church is going to be a viable voice for inclusion, compassion, and hope in today's world.

NOTES

1. Langston Hughes, "Mother to Son."
2. Ibid.
3. Zora Neale Hurston, *Their Eyes Were Watching God* (New York: Harper and Row Perennial Library, 1990), 14.
4. Gospel song, Civilla Martin and Charles Gabriel, 1905.
5. Margaret Busby, ed., *Daughters of Africa* (New York: Pantheon Books, 1992), 300.
6. Maria Stewart, *America's First Black Woman Political Writer*, ed. Marilyn Richardson (Bloomington, IN: Indiana University Press, 1987), 21.
7. Ibid., 30.

8. Alice Walker, *In Search of Our Mothers' Gardens* (New York: Harcourt Brace Jovanovich, 1983), 242–43.

9. Negro Spiritual.

10. Clifton H. Johnson, ed., *God Struck Me Dead: Religious Conversion Experiences and Autobiographies of Ex-Slaves* (Philadelphia and Boston: Pilgrim Press, 1969), 172.

11. bell hooks, *Sisters of the Yam: Black Women and Self-Recovery* (Boston: South End Press, 1993), 8.

12. See Walker, *In Search of Our Mothers' Gardens*, 234,

13. e. e. cummings, "i am a little church," *Complete Poems 1904–1962* (New York: Liveright 1994).

14. Walker, *In Search of Our Mother's Gardens.*

15. Langston Hughes, "Mother to Son."

16. Stewart, *America's First Black Woman Political Writer,* 16.

17. Ibid., 19.

18. See Delores Williams, *Sisters in the Wilderness* (Maryknoll, NY: Orbis Books, 1993), chap. 6.

19. See the Gospel Song, "Please Be Patient with Me," by Sam Wilson.

20. *Sister, Outsider: Essays and Speeches* (Freedom, CA: The Crossing Press, 1984), 114.

21. Emilie Townes, *In a Blaze of Glory: Womanist Spirituality as Social Witness* (Nashville, TN: Abingdon Press, 1995), 10–11.

22. *Trouble Don't Last Always* (Collegeville, MN: Liturgical Press, 1995).

23. *Forged in the Fiery Furnace* (Maryknoll, NY: Orbis Books, 2012).

24. Howard Thurman, *Deep River and the Negro Spiritual Speaks of Life and Death* (Richmond, IN: Friends United Press, 1975).

25. Colleen M. Griffith, ed., *Prophetic Witness: Catholic Women's Strategies for Reform* (New York: Crossroad, 2009), 3.

To Be Black, Catholic, and Female

What does it mean to be a black Catholic woman in the Roman Catholic Church today? In order to answer that question, I must first ask what it means to be black in the church today. The second question necessarily comes first because, not just in the church in the United States but in this society as well, it has always been one's race, if it is other than white, that is first noticed, raised up, remarked upon, questioned or in some other tangible or intangible way made present before any other attributes.

To be black in the United States is to be an anomaly in many ways. It is to be invisible while, at the same time, being denied the peaceful anonymity that should come with invisibility. It is a strange invisibility: your blackness is ignored by others, they walk and talk around it, yet by their very behavior toward you, you realize that they are very much aware, almost painfully aware, of your presence and your difference. It is as Ralph Ellison wrote in his work, *Invisible Man,* so many years ago:

This essay was first published in *New Theology Review* (May 1993): 52–62.

I am an invisible man. No, I am not a spook like those
who haunted Edgar Allan Poe... I am a man of substance, of flesh and bone, fiber and liquids—and I
might even be said to possess a mind. I am invisible,
understand, simply because people refuse to see me.
Like the bodiless heads you see sometimes in circus
sideshows, it is as though I have been surrounded by
mirrors of hard, distorting glass. When people approach me they see only my surroundings, themselves,
or figments of their imagination—indeed, everything
and anything except me.[1]

It is somewhat like being the emperor without any clothes:
everyone nods, smiles, and chatters on with strained looks but
no one has the courage to say the obvious—you are black!
What are you doing here in our midst, purporting to be an educated, intelligent person? Or else they say or insinuate, you're
black but... You don't fit the stereotypes. You're different.

To be black in America is to live in a state of almost perma-
nent paranoia, or so it seems, wondering if what you sense and
feel and see really exists or is just your imagination, even while
you know deep down—because so many others have so many
times experienced the behaviors, the actions, the looks—that
yes, it is the reality. You are not paranoid; you are simply black.
Yet you are also an American because you were born and raised
in the United States; English is your native language; you have
no accent. Still, there is always that question on people's faces
when first they meet you: not who, but what are you—a question I heard repeatedly while studying in Belgium. As W. E. B.
Du Bois noted:

It is a peculiar sensation, this double consciousness, this
sense of always looking at one's history through the
eyes of others, of measuring one's soul by the tape of a

world that looks on in amused contempt and pity. One
ever feels his (or her) twoness—an American, a Negro;
two souls, two thoughts, two unreconciled strivings;
two warring ideals in one dark body, whose dogged
strength alone keeps it from being torn asunder.[2]

Then we must add to blackness another factor, that I am
also Catholic, and my situation becomes even more interesting.
Why would any black person be a Catholic? This question is
asked of me repeatedly as if one chooses Catholicism like one
chooses a new pair of shoes which, upon proving to be too
tight or otherwise not a good fit, can be simply discarded or
traded in for something else.

Most Catholics, including those who are black, do not
know the history of their church or the origins of their faith.
They are woefully ignorant of the fact that black Africans have
been Christian since Christianity's earliest beginnings. As
Cyprian Davis notes:

> Long before Christianity arrived in the Scandinavian
> countries, at least a century before St. Patrick evangel-
> ized Ireland, and over two centuries before St. Augus-
> tine would arrive in Canterbury, and almost seven
> centuries before the conversion of the Poles and the
> establishment of the kingdom of Poland, this moun-
> tainous black kingdom (Ethiopia) was a Catholic na-
> tion with its own liturgy, its own spectacular religious
> art, its own monastic tradition, its saints and its own
> spirituality.[3]

The story in the Acts of the Apostles of the Ethiopian eu-
nuch, who was one of the first converts to Christianity, apparently makes no impression on the Catholic majority. To be black
and Catholic in the United States is seen as a contradiction, a

paradox, some sort of mistake. Many see the 3.1 million plus blacks now in the Catholic Church in this country as somehow temporary aberrations despite the fact that the great majority of them have been Catholic for generations here in the United States dating back to the sixteenth century.

I have always felt at somewhat of a disadvantage when the question of the black presence in the church is raised, because I actually am a convert to the Catholic faith from the African Methodist Episcopal Zion Church. Although a faith-filled person all my life, it was, and still is, in the Catholic Church that I found (or perhaps re-found is better) God, a God who called me forth into the church and challenged me to attempt things I was unaware that I was capable of doing.

What, then, does it mean for me to be a black Catholic woman in the Roman Catholic Church today? Having addressed the questions of what it means to be a black person in this country and a black person in the Roman Catholic Church, I can now turn to the question of what it means to be a woman in the Roman Catholic Church. However, I am not just a woman in the Catholic Church. I am a lay black Catholic female theologian, some would say an "affirmative action dream." But in so saying, it is often tempting to look at only the positive aspects of that dream and to ignore the negative aspects of the accompanying nightmare.

My presence, since 1979, in the Catholic Church has been one of constant challenge, both for myself and for those with whom I have come into contact. I have been challenged, in many ways, to prove not only the legitimacy of my existence but also the validity of my existence in the face of so many others who are not like me at all. As a black, Catholic theologian who is very much a woman, I am, in many ways, doubly if not triply oppressed. It has been a constant struggle, therefore, for me to define not only who but whose I am. That struggle has included finding, acknowledging, and eventually rejoicing in my own voice, a voice unlike anyone else's because it arises out of the very depths of my being—of who I am as black, as Catholic, and as a woman and vowed celibate.

Black feminist bell hooks asserts:

> For women within oppressed groups who have contained so many feelings—despair, rage, anguish—who do not speak, as poet Audre Lorde writes, "for fear our words will not be heard or welcomed," coming to voice is an act of resistance. Speaking becomes both a way to engage in active self-transformation and a rite of passage where one moves from being object to being subject. Only as subjects can we speak. As objects, we remain voiceless—our beings defined and interpreted by others.[4]

As I began to pursue my theological studies, I began to realize that I had been an object for most of my life, defined by society, either male or white, and punished or condemned if I dared to step out of the bounds that had been set for me. Going to law school was my first breaching of those lines. But entering theological studies at the Catholic University of America led to those boundaries being totally shattered.

I did not realize when I first applied for admission to the pontifical program of study that I was treading on new ground. The realization that I was the first laywoman and the first black to enter this program (which confers, after a minimum of seven years of study, the Doctor of Sacred Theology degree) came as a complete shock, not only to me but to many, if not most, of my classmates and a few of my professors, some of whom were not quite prepared for or happy about the presence of a woman in their class. Being new to Catholicism and one who had always enjoyed studying, yet unsure of where my call was going to lead me, I only knew that I wanted the best foundation in theology that I could obtain. The pontifical program with its many required courses and its emphasis on preparing you to teach in every area of theology seemed to me the most logical and appropriate program to embark upon, and so I did. I persisted, despite efforts—some subtle and some not so—to persuade me to settle for the PhD. As a result of that decision, I found myself to be in the distinct minority in all of my classes, whether at Catholic University of America or at the Catholic University of Louvain (Belgium) where I completed my doctorate.

Again, I found myself confronted with questions that, on the surface, seemed innocent enough but always seemed to have an underlying current to them. The most common was: What do you plan to do with your degree? This question was usually posed in a tone of voice accompanied by a peculiar expression that made me feel like a child being asked what I wanted to do when I grew up. This question bothered me for several reasons. First, the underlying, almost cynical, assumption that this was just a game, a passing whim; that I was wasting people's time and taking up space and scholarship funds that should rightly have gone to someone else, preferably male and white. The question was also often accompanied by the unvoiced insinuation that my real reason for studying theology was to find a husband, to be stolen from among the unwary seminarians and priests with whom I studied. The fact that few, if any, were black and all were much younger than I was blithely ignored.

But the question also bothered me because it went to the heart of my own dilemma. As I started out on this journey, I had absolutely no idea how it would end. It was a journey of faith in response to a call from God who had asked me only to begin but had not told me what the end would be. So, for eight years I grappled with that question while fending off others. No, I have no desire to be a priest, although I strongly support women's ordination. No, I have no interest in being a religious, although I made my own personal vow of celibacy at the age of ten and have kept that vow ever since.

I invariably answered the question of my future by stating that I would teach, assuming that the message would get clearer somewhere along the line. And slowly it did, although there are still quite a few foggy patches. I am a theologian, a womanist theologian, in the service of God, my faith, and my church, the Catholic Church.

What does all this mean for me or for those who would follow me as a woman active in the church today? I believe it means that we must recognize that the church is a human institution with the failings and successes found in all human organizations. The church is a reflection of American society, which sadly is still racist and sexist in many ways. Therefore, be prepared to be challenged constantly. It never ends, not even after the degree is earned, the teaching or other position is attained, and the articles and books are written. Being a woman active in the church today requires a deep and abiding faith in a God who loves and can be leaned on during the bad times. It also requires knowledge, for, in the words of Audre Lorde,

> those of us who stand outside the circle of this society's definition of acceptable women; those of us who have been forged in the crucibles of difference—those of us who are poor, who are lesbians, who are Black, who are older—know that *survival is not an academic skill.* It is learning how to stand alone, unpopular and sometimes reviled, and how to make common cause with those others identified as outside the structures in order to define and seek a world in which we can all flourish.[5]

There have been many good times when I feel my efforts are worthwhile and, as well, many bad times when I feel that all

I do is in vain. I have felt, many times, like giving up because of the callous insensitivity of those of my own faith and too often my own race, who are unable to see beyond their own limited experiences to the gift of difference that I can offer. There have also been times, however, when I rejoice at the light of understanding breaking forth on the faces of those with whom I am engaged in dialogue about the need for systemic changes to take place in this church which we love, changes that go to the very core of what it means to be truly Catholic.

I believe that is why I see myself as a liberation theologian, one who does not simply seek to break new ground but who helps others to realize that that ground is not so new but is at the very foundation of our Catholic and Christian faith. Today, as I reread what I wrote so many years ago, I recognize that I was speaking from a womanist context even though that context was, as yet, not fully defined. As a womanist, my concern was for the re-building of the black community and the uplift of its members, regardless of religious creed, gender, class, or sexual orientation. Thus, my life and work were and are today grounded in the historical and cultural experiences of persons of African descent and their encounter with God.

My experience in the Roman Catholic Church has been that of a woman who is an enigma, even a threat, to some because they cannot label me. I do not fit their neatly labeled boxes, whether as black, as female, or as Catholic. I refuse to be labeled. Instead, I am about the business of constantly re-inventing myself as the subject of my own, not someone else's history.

After surviving classes where my questions were ignored or laughed at or where I had to speak as the voice of all women or all blacks, I am now learning simply to be myself, working with language and patterns of writing and speech that are uniquely my own.

After taking the same courses and programs as my male classmates and watching their achievements noted by elaborate celebrations marking their advancement toward ordination while I simply picked up another degree and kept on moving up, unnoticed and uncelebrated, I have learned to reward myself for achieving my own self-determined goals and to proclaim my own celebrations of my rites of passage in life.

As a woman, I have had to sit through a class on the sacrament of reconciliation as a passive witness, forbidden to be confessor or confessee, because of a professor's barely concealed misogyny.

As a black woman, I have had the contributions of my ancestors to the development of Christianity overlooked, ignored, and denied despite my efforts to bring them to light, often at the risk of my grades and professional status.

As a laywoman, I have found myself ostracized by priests and religious, male and female, black and white, because I did not belong to the "club" and was, therefore, not to be trusted and was seen as a possible threat to authority and position.

As a lay black Catholic female theologian, a womanist theologian, however, I have found myself free to challenge, to question, to probe, to define, to teach and be taught, to serve as a loving thorn in the church's side which, hopefully, cannot be removed but serves as a constant reminder of the sins still too prevalent in our midst, the sins of racism, sexism, classism, heterosexism, ableism, and clericalism. I have been free to work with those of open mind and soul toward that "new world a'bornin," one that will not dehumanize or desensitize but give new life and value to all living things.

Being an affirmative action dream obviously has two sides. The down side is that one is always being second-guessed, that one's ability, achievements, knowledge, and presence are too often seen as mere tokenism. If I were to allow myself to accept that assessment of myself, I would be rendered dumb, neutral, of little value to myself or to anyone else. But the upside is that I am free to do and to be whatever God calls me to do and be, free in the knowledge that I went through a portion of hell to get to where I am today and after that, nothing is too hard. I see myself, as I see all women, as a survivor, one who has achieved despite it all. Gay Wilentz affirms that women, especially black women, nurture new worlds into being. They are the bearers of culture, the tellers of the old, old stories and the singers of the old, old songs. I am simply one in a succession of women who have survived, and I believe that it is part of my mandate to ensure that other young women, of whatever race, do likewise. The value of my experience lies in this: that I can pass on the story of my journey to those who come after me so that they, too, will emerge as free, independent, and articulate women of God.

NOTES

1. *The Invisible Man* (New York: Random House, 1972), 3.

2. W. E. B. Du Bois, *The Souls of Black Folk* (New York: Penguin Group Signet Classic, 1995), 45.

3. Cyprian Davis, OSB, "Black Spirituality: A Catholic Perspective," in *One Faith, One Lord, One Baptism: The Hopes and Experiences of the Black Community in the Archdiocese of New York,* vol. 2 (New York: Archdiocese of New York, Office of Pastoral Research,1988), 45.

4. bell hooks, *Talking Back: Thinking Feminist, Thinking Black* (Boston: South End Press, 1989), 12.

5. Audre Lorde, *Sister, Outsider* (Freedom, CA: Crossing Press, 1984), 112.

2

Slain in the Spirit

Black Americans and the Holy Spirit

When beginning to think about how I wanted to approach the understanding of the Holy Spirit from the perspective of African Americans, the words of an old slave spiritual began to run through my mind. Over and over again, I heard words that spelled out the faith of a people in the process of creation, emerging from a past hidden and forbidden to them in Africa, and looking ahead to a new beginning in a strange land over-shadowed by the knowledge that they were welcome only for the quality of their labor rather than the value of their lives.

They sang, in times of trouble, in moments of doubt, words that buoyed them up because they were carried on the wings of a faith which sustained and nurtured them, a faith rich in its West African origins yet interwoven with a new under-standing. They sang:

> *Sometimes I feel discouraged*
> *And think my work's in vain*
> *But then the Holy Spirit*
> *Revives my soul again.*

This article was first published in the *Journal of the Interdenominational Theological Center* (January 1992: 97–115).

> *There is a Balm in Gilead*
> *To make the wounded whole,*
> *There is a Balm in Gilead*
> *To heal the sin-sick soul.*[1]

They sang in witness of, in joyful proclamation of their belief in a God who saves, in a God who lived and died for them, in a God who had sent God's spirit to be with them to affirm them in their conviction that they were a part of God's creation, meant to live a life that was good in God's eyes as free men and women.

Robert Hood sets forth the pervasive force of the Spirit's presence in the life of black Americans in this way:

> The Spirit experientially and conceptually exercises a very strong influence in black American religion and culture . . . Like the breath of God in Scripture, this power moves through slave songs and gospel hymns, the rhetoric of the black preacher and the black trickster alike, the extemporaneous and unrehearsed prayers of the unsophisticated, and the written liturgical prayers of more sedate congregations. It is the presence of the Spirit—revealed in the sounds and ritual of black churches—that impresses black folk at a service, prayer meeting, Bible class, or a revival. With the Spirit present they can say with great sagacity and joy that they "really are in church" or are in "spirit-filled worship."[2]

What are the origins of this conceptualization of the Holy Spirit for African Americans? Its roots are African and are shared by all who are members of the African diaspora. It is the sharing of a common spirit, "an attitude that sees all of life in the context of the encounter with the Divine, and the all-embracing vision of the Divine-human encounter."[3] It is grounded in a world-view (recognizing that African traditions and religions vary) that emphasizes the community as the basic source of identity and spirituality.

> Besides belief in a Supreme Being, the African religious traditions emphasize belief in the ancestors, the practice of sacrifice, belief in spirits and powers (both good and evil), and, finally, belief in the fullness of the present life. Reverence for ancestors, in particular, is a universally important feature of African religions... The Spirit of the ancestors is a vital part of the African concept of community, in which the collective power of all members of the community—the living and the "living dead" —energizes and pervades the daily life of everyone.[4]

Of singular importance for African religion is the "preservation and strengthening of life-force or power" which serves as its organizing principle. This power was manifested for good and evil through gods and spirits.

> The gods and men related to one another through the mediation of sacrifice, the mechanism of divination, and through the phenomenon of spirit possession. Widely shared by diverse West African societies were several fundamental beliefs concerning the relationship of the divine and the human: belief in a transcendent and benevolent God, creator and ultimate source of providence; belief in a number of immanent gods, to whom people must sacrifice in order to make life propitious; belief in the power of the spirits animating things in nature to affect the welfare of people; belief in priests and others who were expert in practical knowledge of the

gods and spirits; belief in spirit possession, in which gods, through their devotees, spoke to men.[5]

This worldview, with its emphasis on the continuity of the spiritual and physical realms, traveled with the captive Africans to their new homes in the Americas. There, in the clash between their indigenous faith and the Christianity that was forced upon them, a new spirituality emerged, but one that also retained many of the religious traditions that had shaped and formed them as a living community of faith in their homeland. As Raboteau notes, the African gods were "carried in the memories of enslaved Africans across the Atlantic" and were revealed especially in such African American religions as Candomble, Santeria, and Vodun—syncretistic meshings of traditional African religions and the Catholic faith. Catholicism was especially open to such meshings as the slaves experienced a correlation between their gods and spirits and Catholic saints as well as other Catholic symbols and rituals which were not present in Protestantism with its relative lack of ritual and symbolism.

It is in the development of what has come to be called "slave religion" that we encounter many of the Africanisms that were retained. In its expression of religious emotion, certain forms and manners are clearly reminiscent of African religious expressions. I would like to explore, as an example, "spirit possession" or, as it is more commonly referred to in the black church in the United States, being "slain in the spirit." Raboteau states that there is a "discontinuity... between the African heritage of spirit possession and the Black shouting tradition in the United States."[6] Yet, at the same time a continuity can be seen "in the context of action, the patterns of motor behavior preceding and following the ecstatic experience."[7] Both traditions involve "hand clapping, foot-rapping, rhythmic preaching, hyperventilation, antiphonal (call and response) singing and dancing. Only the drums were missing initially in the United States, but these have in recent years re-emerged along with brass and wind instruments, guitars, piano, organ, tambourines, and other instrumental forms of "making a joyful noise unto the Lord."[8]

> The preacher was drawing his sermon to a close ... [w]hen a small old woman ... among those in the gallery, suddenly rose and began dancing and clapping her hands; at first with a slow and measured movement, and then with increasing rapidity, at the same time beginning to shout "ha! ha!" The women about her arose also, and tried to hold her ... The woman was still shouting and dancing, her head thrown back and rolling from one side to the other. Gradually her shout became indistinct, she threw her arms wildly about instead of clapping her hands, fell back into the arms of her companions, then threw herself forward and embraced those before her, then tossed herself from side to side, gasping, and finally sunk to the floor, where she remained ... kicking, as if acting a death struggle.[9]

Thus, on a physical level both traditions are rather similar, but on the theological level significantly different. In the African tradition, devotees of a particular god or gods are possessed by that god or those gods "whose personality displaces that of the human medium which has no self-control."[10] However, in black Christianity, "it is the context of belief [which] shapes the possession experience and determines the manner in which the experience is interpreted."[11] Rather than being "mounted" and "ridden" by a god or gods, it is instead "the Holy Spirit who fills the converted sinner with a happiness and power that drives him to shout, sing and sometimes dance."[12]

The old meeting house caught on fire. The spirit was there. Every heart was beating in unison as we turned our minds to God to tell him of our sorrows here below. God saw our need and came to us. I used to wonder what made people shout but now I don't. There is a joy on the inside and it wells up so strong that we can't keep still. It is fire in the bones. Any time that fire touches a man, he will jump.[13]

It is the belief, the faith context, which is different. "While the North American slaves danced under the impulse of the Spirit of a 'new' God, they danced in ways their fathers in Africa would have recognized."[14]

It is in the narratives the slaves themselves told of their conversion experiences that this shift is clearly seen. The African slaves were taught a distorted Christianity which mandated their oppression and denied their humanity yet, paradoxically, they were able to discern the kernel of truth in Jesus' message—that God was a God for all, and that all of God's creation was good. Their conversion experience confirmed this goodness within them in ways that dramatically contrasted their physical status of enslavement with their spiritual breaking of the chains that bound them.

To be converted meant "getting religion"—being "slain in the Spirit"—"struck dead" by the hand of God and revived as a new being. It was a physical, rather than passive act, in which the spirit led them to shout, speak of visions of God, heaven, or freedom and engage in often frenzied behavior that "manifested the Spirit's presence."[15]

One's true rather than slave identity was revealed through conversion, the revelation that one was a "child of God . . . a human being, one of those redeemed by God"[16] and it was the Spirit of the Lord Jesus Christ who showed the path to that new identity. George Cummings notes that:

The Spirit's presence, according to [an ex-slave named Cornelius] Garner, entailed the affirmation of independence and selfhood, sustained hope for freedom as embodied in their prayer life; served as the basis of love within the slave community; and even assisted slaves in their desire to escape to freedom. The Spirit's sustaining power/presence was nurtured in the secret meetings where Black slaves disobeyed their masters' orders to serve God, sustained their sense of personal identity and well-being, and provided mutual support for each other by giving meaning and hope to their tragic existence.[17]

Sarah Rhodes, a former slave, speaks of those meetings in this way:

> We used to steal off to de woods and have church, like de Spirit moved us—sing and pray to our own liking and soul satisfaction—and we sure did have good meetings, honey-baptize in de river like God said. We had dem spirit-filled meetings at night on de bank of de river and God met us there.[18]

Their defiance was born of the Spirit which moved them to disobey their masters in order to obey their God, a God whom they knew had created them as free men and women in God's own Spirit. This Spirit-grounded strength enabled them to flee plantations, plot and carry out escapes and rebellions, and silently but obstinately refuse to participate in their own dehumanization, often to the consternation and fear of their masters.

The slave narratives reveal an eschatological hope which reflects "a connection between the presence of the Spirit of God and the hopes and aspirations of the slave community."[19] Theirs was a hope born of a burning desire for freedom and the determination to one day be free. It was an eschatological hope born of the Spirit's movement within them and the Spirit's sustaining and nurturing presence in every aspect of their lives.

They looked forward to a reversal of the status quo—a shift in time and situation for them and those who oppressed them, expressed in the belief that "everybody talking about heaven am not going there." The future was promised them and gave them the ability to stay strong, but it was not a future way off somewhere. It was, at one and the same time, here but not yet in its fullness. The "eschaton was not an opiate. The transcendent future was also the present. The 'home over yonder' and the 'promised land' of the spirituals were for the slaves both an 'otherworldly' promise and a 'this worldly' hope for freedom."[20]

The spirituals spoke of a future freedom to come in heaven, but one that could also be achieved by their actions in escaping to the North and to Canada, in fighting against their oppressed status. The spirituals are the voice of the Spirit of God expressed in the words of an illiterate yet faith-filled people. James Cone sees the Spirit as

> God himself breaking into the lives of the people, "building' them up where they were torn down and proppin' them up on every leanin' side." The Spirit was God's presence with the people and his will to provide them the courage and the strength to make it through.[21]

They could, therefore, sing in affirmation of that presence: "Every time I feel the Spirit moving in my heart I will pray." For it was a feeling, a feeling reflected in rhythm, in song, and in faith. "This song invites the believer to move close to the very sources of black being, and to experience the black community's power to endure and the will to survive.[22]

All the believer has to do is to respond to the divine apocalyptic disclosure of God's revelation and cry, "Have mercy, please." This cry is not a cry of passivity, but a faithful, free response to the movement of the Black Spirit. It is the Black community accepting themselves as the people of the Black Spirit and knowing through his presence that no chains can hold the Spirit of black humanity in bondage.[23]

Cone concludes that "the spiritual, then, is the Spirit of the people struggling to be free."[24] He continues:

Black history then is the stuff out of which the black spirituals were created. But the "stuff" of black history includes more than the bare historical facts of slavery. Black history is an experience, a soulful event. And to understand it is to know the being of a people who had to "feel their way along the course of American slavery," enduring the stresses and strains of human servitude but not without a song. Black history is a spiritual.[25]

It is the sung-memory of a hope sustained against all odds for a freedom that will come, in God's own time and their own. This eschatological hope and their acting upon it had the effect of transforming them, not just spiritually but also in physical ways. As Harriet Tubman noted: "I looked at my hands to see if I was de same person now I was free. Dere was such a glory ober de fields and I felt like I was in heaven."[26]

This experience of the working of the Spirit continues to be a part of black America's understanding of how God acts in their history. It calls forth "a spirituality that is not the classic *imitati Christi*, but rather *participati Christi*, through performance, drama, emotion and ritual."[27]

As slavery gave way to a "putative" freedom, the Spirit remained with the people, revealing itself in ways that continued
to affirm and strengthen them in their positive self-understanding of themselves as a people of a loving and liberating God. The
Spirit sustained them over against the stereotypical depictions
and degradations they were forced to endure in their daily lives.

W. E. B. Du Bois, although deploring, as did many educated and middle class blacks, the emotionality and noisiness of
his brothers' and sisters' witnessing to the Spirit's movement
within them, nevertheless, recognized the Spirit as one of the
hallmarks of black religion:

> It varies in expression from the silent rapt countenance
> or the low murmur and moan to the mad abandon of
> physical fervor—the stomping, shrieking and shouting,
> the rushing to and fro and wild waving of arms, the
> weeping and laughter, the vision and the trance, All
> this is nothing new in the world, but old as religion, as
> Delphi and Endor. And so firm a hold did it have on
> the Negro that many generations have firmly believed
> that without this visible manifestation of God there
> could be no true communion with the Invisible.[28]

Many class-conscious blacks opposed this "exhibition," as
they saw it, as being primitive and heathenish, preferring the
staid, sedate, unmoved and unmoving rituals and services of
predominately white churches. Today, this attitude is changing
as blacks in the Episcopal, Roman Catholic, and other mainline
churches are returning to their roots in the African American
community—a community brought into existence by the action
of the Spirit shaping, forming, nurturing, and sustaining an oppressed and beleaguered people. More and more middle class
African Americans are seeking that which they have lost some-

where along the way up. They are recognizing and reaffirming a heritage almost irreclaimable and certainly abandoned in favor of a form of assimilation which often led to self-denial and alienation. Roman Catholics particularly are realizing that Spirit-induced fervor is a part of both their African and Catholic heritages as evidenced by the Catholic mission of the nineteenth century. In its day that mission was comparable to a Protestant revival and was a means of evangelizing both blacks and whites.

Catholics looked down upon the Protestant form of revivalism, especially Methodist camp meetings, as "heathenish" assemblies. The Catholic clergy opposed religious enthusiasm as an end in itself. It was felt that, "in Protestant revivals, excitement is carried to excess, and made the end aimed at. In Catholic retreats and missions, it is wisely managed and made simply a means."[29] In actuality, they were not that different.

As with the camp meetings, often the parish mission was held wherever a large group of people could be congregated. On the frontier, this meant huge tents, open fields, or barns. Both aimed for conversion, the reclaiming of sinners for Jesus Christ, and were "specially calculated to excite the piety of the faithful."[30] Stress was on the spoken word, often accompanied by a "variety of theatrical techniques." The mission was preached with "powerful emotion," and often the audiences responded with spontaneous outbursts of weeping, shuddering, and moaning. Catholic revival preachers were also itinerant circuit riders. Initially, emphasis was on the already baptized but fallen away Catholics. The revival was an occasion for conversion of the indifferent, the new immigrants who had recently arrived from Europe and who were failing rapidly in their faith.

The Paulist order was the first indigenous religious order in the United States established specifically to run parish missions. The Paulists emphasized that:

> A mission . . . is something which gathers into one powerful showing all the warnings of Divine Justice fully explaining the enormous folly and ingratitude of sin; it leads the sinner back to his very childhood and traces his downward track through youth and manhood towards his last death; which stands with him at his open grave; which calls in his ear the summons to the judgement seat of an offended God; which scorches his face with the fires of hell and all in an atmosphere of fervor, aided by the entreaties of the sinner's friends, their prayers to God, their tears, the example of the repentance of other sinners.[31]

This was evangelicalism in exemplary form. A Redemptorist priest likened the mission "to a thunder and lightning storm" which "bursts upon the scene with powerful sermons to arouse man from the lethargy of sin to a life of fervor."[32] With its emphasis on sin, its stress on fear of the Lord, and its aim of arousing fear, reverence, awe, hatred of sin, and love of God, one can say, quite truthfully, that the parish mission was, indeed, a revival in all but name.

Catholic revivalism, however, was different in its emphasis on turning away from the world and toward more celestial goals. Unlike Evangelical Protestantism, which led to the evolution of the Protestant version of the social gospel with its emphasis on making the world into the Kingdom of God, Catholic evangelicalism removed the Catholic from the world and left him or her concerned only with achieving the afterlife rather than attempting to improve the situation of his or her neighbor.

Another striking characteristic of Catholic evangelicalism was its emphasis on the sacraments and sacramentals. By itself, a personal decision for Christ was considered incomplete. It had to be verified by a "sacramental confession of one's sins and the eventual reception of the Eucharist."[33]

For Catholics salvation was achieved through the instrumentality of the visible Church and its sacraments. The spirit of orthodoxy allowed for no other alternative. Catholic revivalism encouraged a sacramental evangelicalism which not only urged the sinner to repent but also provided the means necessary for such a conversion. For Catholics personal conviction of sin was only the first step toward salvation and without the Church the pursuit of holiness could not be realized.[34]

Nevertheless, for black Christians, Protestant and Catholic, "the Spirit . . . did not have simply an internal or personal function; it also functioned externally and socially. . . [allowing] for defiance as well as [ensuring] confidence and triumph,"[35] and providing empowerment. There was an ethical dimension to the Spirit's presence as well, one which sustained African Americans in their seemingly unending struggle for legitimacy. It also "established a solidarity," a community of faith from within which such a struggle could be maintained. This can be seen most clearly during the period of their struggle for civil rights, where the use of spirituals as well as the more recent gospel music served as a source of encouragement and inspiration.

I believe that James Baldwin gives the most poignant and evocative illustration of the workings of the Holy Spirit, both in building community and in calling forth individuals to leadership within that community. In his autobiographical work, *Go Tell It on the Mountain*, we are introduced to John, a young black male, lost, unsure of himself and of the relevance of the church in his life, angry, rebellious, yet afraid to step out alone. It is here that we can clearly see the continuity, the continuous thread of the Spirit running through the lives of black Americans—from those slaves metaphorically "struck dead" by God to rise with hands, feet, and a heart made new, to the blacks of today, still seeking affirmation of their humanity and still trusting in the Lord.

Baldwin writes: "On the threshing floor, in the center of the crying, praying saints, John lay astonished beneath the power of the Lord." Suddenly, in the middle of a religious service like so many he had attended during his life at this store-front church, John finds himself face down in front of the altar—struck down by God.

Baldwin's graphic description of this encounter with the Holy Spirit re-unites us once again with the African ancestral heritage of spirit possession, of being "slain in the Spirit," of being taken up by the Spirit of God and made God's own.

> He knew, without knowing how it had happened, that he lay on the floor, in the dusty space before the altar which he and Elisha had cleaned; and knew that above him burned the yellow light which he had himself switched on. Dust was in his nostrils, sharp and terrible, and the feet of the saints, shaking the floor beneath him, raised small clouds of dust that filmed his mouth. He heard their cries, so far, so high above him—he could never rise that far. He was like a rock, a dead man's body, a dying bird, fallen from an awful height; something that had no power of itself, any more, to turn.

> And something moved in John's body which was not John. He was invaded, set at naught, possessed. This power had struck John, in the head or in the heart; and, in a moment, wholly, filling him with an anguish that he could never in his life have imagined, that he surely could not endure, that even now he could not believe, had opened him up; had cracked him open, as wood beneath the axe cracks down the middle, as rocks break up; had ripped him and felled him in a moment, so that John had not felt the wound, but only the agony, had not felt the fall, but only the fear; and lay

here, now, helpless, screaming, at the very bottom of darkness.[36]

John struggles through, urged on by the prayers of the saints, the community in which he has grown and matured and which continues to watch over him as he fights for his very soul, trembling in fear and anger as memories—both pleasant and painful—ravage him and an ironic voice tempts him to rise and walk away. Yet he finds that he cannot rise, that he does not want to rise, not until he has called upon the Lord for mercy and love and has prayed for God's help in "coming through," passing over to the other side—into the light of a new life. Baldwin continues:

And someone cried: "Sinner, do you love my Lord!' Then John saw the Lord—for a moment only; and the darkness, for a moment only, was filled with a light he could not bear. Then, in a moment, he was set free; his tears sprang as from a fountain; his heart, like a fountain of waters, burst. Then he cried: "Oh, blessed Jesus! OH, Lord Jesus! Take me through."

Of tears there was, yes a very fountain—springing from a depth never sounded before, from depths John had not known were in him. And he wanted to rise up, singing, singing in that great morning, the morning of his new life. Ah, how his tears ran down, how they blessed his soul!—as he felt himself, out of the darkness, and the fire, and the terrors of death, rising upward to meet the saints.

"Oh, yes!" cried the voice of Elisha. "Bless our God forever."

And a sweetness filled John as he heard this voice, and heard the sound of singing: the singing was for him. For his soul was anchored in the love of God; in the rock that endured forever. The light and the darkness had kissed each other, and were married now, forever, in the life and the vision of John's soul.[37]

Today, the Spirit is still with black Americans in their state of oppression and marginalization in the United States. She is manifested in word and deed, in song and prayer, in all of the myriad forms that a creative people have employed to evoke her presence in good times and bad. The Spirit continues to live out God's promise to God's people to sustain them in their faithful journeying toward that new dispensation where they too will be free of the "troubles of the world."

The Spirit still works to build and maintain community even in the midst of apparent fragmentation. The black church, that body of all believers of African descent in the United States, stands united across denominational lines and class barriers to witness to the Spirit's life-giving and empowering presence in the ghettoes and barrios of our inner cities, serving as a challenging beacon of hope and an island of refuge in the midst of a seeming wasteland. The Spirit of God "dispels weariness and faintheartedness. It connects ancestors with the living, mothers with sons, daughters with fathers, the uneducated with the sophisticated, and the impoverished with the affluent."[38]

It is building new communities, rejoining the scattered members of the African diaspora both within and outside the United States, affirming them in their shared oppression, but also leading them forward out of that oppression to new heights expressed in a renaissance of black culture and the continuing development of black theology.

Major Jones summarizes well the role that the Holy Spirit has played in the lives of African Americans, both past and present:

During the bitter times, the Holy Spirit, God's inner agent—inner to God and inner within us—played the decisive role. It was the Holy Spirit who called, compelled, gathered, restrained, disciplined, and sanctified. It was the Holy Spirit who became our fortress against despair, defeatism, and deep-festering hate. It was the Holy Spirit who first inspired into being the invisible Black Church of Jesus Christ, and then indwelled those Black people of faith and kept the Spirit of Truth about themselves alive within them. It was the holy and personal presence of God's Spirit that affirmed the integrity of Black people's personhood and the legitimacy of their humanity, when the White-controlled churches and the larger society were teaching them the falsehoods of subordination and subjection. And it was—and is—the Holy Spirit of everlasting liberty through whom God and Jesus Christ stood in unmitigated opposition against every form and expression of race evil, human disregard, and personal insult. The times are not yet perfect, but they are better because of the work of Jesus Christ and the Holy Spirit.[39]

I have, however, chosen for the last words of this discourse on the Holy Spirit, a statement from an anonymous freed woman who said: "I have seen nothing nor heard nothing, but only felt the Spirit in my soul, and I believe that will save me when I come to die."[40]

NOTES

1. Negro Spiritual.
2. Robert E. Hood, *Must God Remain Greek? Afro Cultures and God-Talk* (Minneapolis: Augsburg Fortress, 1990), 204.
3. Jamie Phelps, OP, "Black Spirituality," in Robin Maas and Gabriel O'Donnell, OP, eds., *Spiritual Traditions for the Contemporary Church* (Nashville: Abingdon Press, 1990), 332.

4. Ibid., 335.

5. Albert Raboteau, *Slave Religion: The "Invisible" Institution in the Antebellum South* (New York: Oxford University Press, 1978), 11.

6. Ibid., 64.

7. Ibid., 62.

8. Ibid.

9. Ibid.

10. Ibid., 63.

11. Ibid., 64.

12. Ibid.

13. Clifton H. Johnson, *God Struck Me Dead: Religious Conversion Experiences and Autobiographies of Ex-Slaves* (Philadelphia: Pilgrim Press, 1969), 74.

14. Raboteau, *Slave Religion*, 72.

15. George Cummings, "The Slave Narratives as a Source of Black Theological Discourse: The Spirit and Eschatology" in *Cut Loose Your Stammering Tongue: Black Theology in the Slave Narratives*, ed. Dwight N. Hopkins and George Cummings (Maryknoll, NY: Orbis, 1991), 48.

16. Ibid., 48–49.

17. Ibid., 49.

18. James Mellon, *Bullwhip Days: The Slaves Remember* (New York: Weidenfeld and Nicolson, 1988), 194–95.

19. Cummings, "The Slave Narratives," 54.

20. Ibid., 58.

21. James Cone, *The Spirituals and the Blues: An Interpretation* (New York: Crossroad/Seabury Press, 1972; Maryknoll, NY: Orbis Books, 1991), 2.

22. Ibid., 5.

23. Ibid.

24. Ibid., 32.

25. Ibid., 33.

26. Sarah Bradford, *Harriet Tubman: The Moses of Her People* (New York: Corinth Books, 1961), 30.

27. Hood, *Must God Remain Greek?* 205.

28. W. E. B. Du Bois, *The Souls of Black Folk* (Greenwich, CT: Fawcett Publications, 1961), 141–42.

29. Diana L. Hayes, "Black Catholic Revivalism: The Emergence of a New Form of Worship," *Journal of the Interdenominational Theological Center* 14, nos. 1 and 2 (Fall 1986/Spring 1987): 86.

30. Jay P. Dolan, "American Catholics and Revival Religion, 1850–1900," *Horizons* 3 (Spring 1976), 44.

31. Ibid., 46.

32. Ibid., 45.

33. Ibid., 54.

34. Ibid.

35. Hood, *Must God Remain Greek?* 204.

36. James Baldwin, *Go Tell It on the Mountain* (New York: Dell, 1985), 193.

37. Ibid., 204.

38. Hood, *Must God Remain Greek?* 210.

39. Major Jones, *The Color of God: The Concept of God in Afro-American Thought* (Macon, GA: Mercer University Press, 1987), 118–19.

40. Clifton Johnson, *God Struck Me Dead*, 172.

3

Deep River

The Christian Vocation of the Laity

I've known rivers;
I've known rivers ancient as the world and older than the flow of
human blood in human veins.
My soul has grown deep like the rivers.
I bathed in the Euphrates when dawns were young.
I built my hut near the Congo and it lulled me to sleep.
I looked upon the Nile and raised the pyramids above it.
I heard the singing of the Mississippi when Abe Lincoln went
down to New Orleans,
And I've seen its muddy bosom turn all golden in the sunset.
I've known rivers;
Ancient, dusky rivers.
My soul has grown deep like the rivers.

—Langston Hughes[1]

The River of Life

This poem has always, in some mysterious way, haunted me.
Why? I'm not at all sure. Perhaps it's because I've always seen

---

First published *in Spiritual Life* (Fall 1993): 13–36.

life as a river—a river flowing ceaselessly, seeking its end, which paradoxically is also its beginning. Or perhaps it's because I see my own life as a river flowing from and through my parents, grandparents, and beyond, with tributary influences from loving friends and mentoring teachers, with drifts and shallows where I thought I had stopped moving at all, and with sudden rushes and gushes where I thought I would carry away all before me or be swept away myself. My life, our lives, are like rivers. We are rivers, singly and together, together a river of peoples, a river of nations within a nation in these United States of America, and even more so within the church. We are a river flowing to the sea from whence we once came: that sea of endless wonder, that sea of creative force from which we came into being and toward which we spend our lives seeking to return.

Vincent Harding speaks of black history in the United States as a river, but also realizes that analogy has a broader application, for, as he says, "the river is in us, created by us, flowing out of us, surrounding us, recreating us and this entire nation . . . We are . . . the river, and at the same time . . . the river is more than us—generations more, millions more."[2] In our flow through life, that span allotted each of us, whether long or short, is a journey, a river's journey toward the sea, toward the source of our being, toward God. As St. Augustine recognized about his own life, "Thou hast made us for thyself, and our souls are restless till they find their rest in thee." Life is indeed a river.

Shifts in the Flow

A river has many tributaries, many branches, but only one source and only one goal. A river flows, sometimes placidly, sometimes tumultuously, gaining force here, losing it there, but steadily seeking its end. Just as the river, our own lives ebb and flow, gathering force for a while, lying placidly at other times, while we perhaps regain our strength or refind our selves—but always there is a current that flows through us, that guides us, that keeps us on course even when we perversely seek to change course.

Rivers are an important metaphor for me as a layperson, because they speak directly of our lives as laypersons. As laity, we are baptized into the river of Christian life and set forth on that river into the service of God, given different charisms to explore and develop, gifted with tongues or prophecy or teaching or preaching. Some seem blessed with almost all these gifts, while others appear to have very few. But in our seeming meanderings, our wanderings toward what appear to be detours and dead ends, we are all guided to our source, the source that is our Creator God. My life has been a river, a rather eclectic one, with unlikely tributaries and corkscrews and twistings and turnings, from Protestantism to Catholicism, from music to science to law and finally to theology, but always there has been that steady, guiding current leading me on.

All of us, like rivers and their tributaries, may have different twists and turns, may linger in one place or another for a longer or shorter time, picking up different flavors, different colorings, different voices, but eventually we all come together to form that mighty stream of humanity flowing toward God—the eternal answer, as Karl Rahner notes, to which all men and women in their finite existence are the constant, persistent question. As laypersons, our vocations are diverse; they can range in so many directions, some of which seem to have little or nothing to do with our homeward journey in Christ. And yet we are constantly called and guided, often when we least expect or realize it.

Howard Thurman, one of the earliest and least known black theologians of this country, notes that a river "may twist and turn, fall back on itself and start again, stumble over an infinite series of hindering rocks," be dammed up temporarily or thrown off course by cataclysmic upheavals, yet at last "must answer the call of the sea. It is restless till it finds its rest in the sea." As with rivers, so with life: for both, the source and goal are the same.

The goal of life is God! The source of life is God! That
out of which life comes is that into which life goes.
[God] out of whom life comes is [the same God] into
whom life goes. God is the goal of [humanity's] life,
the end of all . . . seeking, the meaning of all . . . striving.
God is the guarantor of all [humanity's] values, the ultimate meaning—the timeless frame oreference.[3]

Therefore, although we may be thrown off course, though
we may wander for what seems like years—in darkness and dis-
array, through sin and despair, war and pestilence, hate and
love—we keep seeking, moving forward, until we find our rest
in the One who created us all.

The Christian Vocation

This talk of rivers may seem to have little bearing on the Christian vocation of the laity, but for me it is fundamental, for even
though we spend our lives working, playing, creating families,
winning or losing, building or tearing down, we are always—
as Christians, as true followers of Christ—seeking the path that
will allow us to flow toward home, toward the sea, toward
God.

The signs have been posted for us, though we too often ignore them; the pathways have been marked, but often we prefer another apparently easier path. As laity, we are supposedly
the "salt of the earth," the "leaven," but we've managed to
produce some pretty flat, stale, and tasteless bread in our haste
and greed to "make it" in this world without considering the
consequences for ourselves and others, let alone for "making it"
in that other world toward which we are bound.

The Lord clearly notes the path that we must take, the bed
that the river of humanity must flow along, in order to truly become one with all humanity and, in time, with God. But too

often we fail to listen, we refuse to hear, we refuse to follow for so many seemingly important reasons. The prophet Isaiah summons us:

> *Wash yourselves clean!*
> *Put away your misdeeds from before my eyes:*
> *Cease doing evil; learn to do good.*
> *Make justice your aim: redress the wronged,*
> *Hear the orphan's plea, defend the widow.*
>
> (Isaiah 1:16–17)

How simple those words sound, yet in practice how difficult! What does it mean "to do good, to seek justice"? My students ask: Must we all become social workers or run shelters for the homeless? No, of course not; the country would not survive if that were the case. The diversity of our lives is important and necessary, but only if within that diversity we recognize our connectedness, that we are "co-created" by Almighty God. It is that co-creation that calls us to live our lives in ways that make a positive difference in our world, regardless of whether we are bankers or paupers, lawyers or preachers, teachers or athletes. The Buddhists speak of "bodhisattvas," those who have almost attained Nirvana but who put off their own attainment in order to help others also achieve that final step. We Christians speak of saints (like Teresa of Avila, Mother Teresa of Calcutta, and others) but too often they are people whose lives seem so far removed from our own that we can never hope to imitate them. Yet look around at those sitting next to us in church, those we meet every day. These are—or can become—true saints, and without our knowing it are perhaps already in the process. They may be simply living out their lives—moving ahead, yes, but not at the expense of others. Rather, they are seeking to bring along with them as many others as they can. Today's saints are those who recognize that they did not get where they are "on their own" (no one does, or none of us would ever be born!), but in the footsteps and on the shoulders of "those generations, those millions," as Harding noted, who have come before them.

We are not alone in this world, nor have we ever been, no matter how much we may feel otherwise. Many have come before us and will come after us feeling the same way, seeking as we are, searching for the "light." And it is in coming to-gether—one by one, two by two, and on and on—that we form the converging tributaries that make up the mighty stream of just and righteous people flowing home to God. We are and can be that justice that "rolls down like water," and that righteousness that "flows like a mighty stream" (Amos 5:24).

This is our calling as Christian faithful: to recognize the Christ in everyone. And to reach out a hand of hope, to speak a word of love, to sing a song of happiness, to share a tear of joy or pain, to speak a word of praise, to murmur a prayer, to stand together against those forces that would divide us, isolate us, and block our flow toward home.

To Do the Right

We must seek to become the righteous of God, recognizing that the path is neither short nor easy, but rock-strewn, obsta-cle-laden, sometimes even seeming to flow backwards and up-hill! But as the prophet Micah proclaims:

> *You have been told ... what is good*
> *And what the Lord requires of you:*
> *Only to do the right and to love goodness,*
> *And to walk humbly with your God.*
> (Micah 6:8)

This is the Christian vocation of the laity in the world. Today and every day. It is not an easy vocation, for there are temptations to flow in other directions, to leave our own course and follow the so-called "main-stream," a stream that appears large and exciting but eventually peters out into nothingness, into unrequited grief and sorrow.

The black scientist George Washington Carver, who was scoffed at for his research on the lowly peanut but whose studies yielded many discoveries beneficial to humanity, stressed that "how far you go in life depends on your being tender with the aged, sympathetic with the striving, and tolerant of the weak and the strong. Because someday in life you will have been all of these." We see the poignant truth of these words where so many among us have fallen, where the "golden dreams" of the 1980s have turned into the leaden balloons of the 1990s. The homeless person we do not notice on the street today, because we turn our heads away, may be the man or woman who last year sat in a conference, restaurant, or office with us—as stockbroker or executive, salesperson or construction worker, a person with a job, home, family, and future—but who now has nothing and without our loving kindness and active aid will always have nothing.

The river is still flowing. We can accept the grace to be part of that flow or we can choose to step outside of it, onto seeming dry land that too often turns out to be quicksand. But if we truly are to be followers of Christ, imitators of him, then we must leap with faith into that torrent, knowing that we are buoyed up on all sides, and will not sink or drown but will come back in time to where we first began, in the bosom of God, our Creator, our Sustainer, our Liberator, our Mother and Father.

A River of Hope

I would like to end with another poem, a song actually, that also speaks of a river, a river of hope. It speaks on many levels, all of which, however, are connected. It is a song that speaks of the determination and belief of a people who in their time of trial and tribulation were still able to wade bravely into the waters of faith in God, as must we all. The song/poem is "Deep River":

Deep River, my home is over Jordan:
Deep River, Lord, I want to cross over
 into campground.
O, don't you want to go to that Gospel feast.
That promised land where all is peace?
Deep River, Lord, I want to cross over
 into campground.[4]

"Campground" is heaven, yes, our home of spiritual salvation, but at one time it was also the North, then the home of physical salvation as well. The two were not seen as opposites but part of a whole; the "end time" was "not yet" here in its fullness, but coming, "already" on its way.

Let us continue to pray and ponder, thinking of the river of our own lives, how it has flowed, where it has been stilled for a while, where it has gushed forth with vigor. Let us reflect on where we are going as individuals, as a people, as a nation; why we seek to go there; and how we are trying to get there. Let us ask ourselves how we can come together to forge a mighty stream that will cleanse and heal, that will purify and carry us home into the arms of our loving God.

For we are all a part of that river flowing to the sea, to our God. Let us allow and encourage our souls to grow deep like the rivers.

NOTES

1. "The Negro Speaks of Rivers," *The Poetry of Black America: Anthology of the Twentieth Centuyr*, ed. Arnold Adoff (New York: Harper and Row, 1973), 72.

2. Vincent Harding, *There Is a River: The Black Struggle for Freedom in America* (New York: Harcourt Brace Jovanovich, 1981), xix.

3. Howard Thurman, *Deep River* (Richmond, IN: Friends United Press, 1975), 76–77.

4. Negro Spiritual.

Trouble Don't Last Always

Soul Prayers

Reality for blacks in the United States has always been one of seeming paradox. "Trouble" always seems to be in our way, regardless of the form it takes, from forced migration, slavery, second-class citizenship, to the constant enervating struggle with proponents of racism and the lack of opportunity for education, decent health care, and a life of dignity and happiness. Yet, through it all or, perhaps it can be said, because of it all, we have been a people with our eyes "fixed" on God, a people for whom "trouble don't last always."

> *Trouble in my way,*
> *I have to cry sometimes.*
> *Trouble in my way,*
> *I have to cry sometimes.*

The spirituals, blues, and other forms of black music that have emerged in the United States are the "soul prayers" of black Americans. Forbidden to read or write, illiterate slaves

---

The prayers in this chapter are taken from *Trouble Don't Last Always* (Collegeville, MN: Liturgical Press, 1995).

wrote their transforming and liberating theologies in the books of their souls and transcribed them in the depths of their hearts, then passed them on, literally, from mouth to mouth, from ear to ear, down through the generations.

This music—once thought to be based on hopes for an eventual, peaceful death and a pleasant life afterwards in a "land flowing with milk and honey" where me and you and "all God's children" would have shoes, warm clothes, and all of the other needful things missing from a life filled with harshness and want—can be seen to be songs not of defeat or acquiescence but of a constant, enduring, burning faith in a God who loves, a God who liberates, a God who acts in history, in the here-and-now of everyday life, to bring about relief from pain, hunger, and oppression.

> *I lay awake at night*
> *But that's alright*
> *I know my Jesus will fix it*
> *After a while.*

My own life has enabled me to follow, at times unwillingly, the struggles of my people and to experience the pain of being "different" in too many ways to make life in this world, with its stress on conformity, an unvarnished blessing.

I grew up the second child in a family of four girls. From the very beginning of my life, I was labeled "different" by a world that did not understand the thirst, the hunger for knowledge that resided within me. Having somehow learned to read by the time I was three years old, I was never satisfied with the "arbitrary" restrictions I felt had been placed on my life by my family's poverty or the fact that I was both black and female at a time when being either or both was seen as of little importance or value.

Yet I persevered in my efforts to be educated, "devouring" most of the books in our neighborhood branch library by the time I was fourteen years old, then walking miles to the downtown library to tap into that seemingly endless source of literary wealth. I loved classical music as well, an interest that bewildered my sisters who were used to listening to rhythm and blues. I was deeply moved by the spirituals and by the soulful strains of jazz, again, tastes no one else in my family seemed to have.

I loved poetry of all kinds, by writers of all races. By the time I finished high school, I had read the Bible in its entirety in at least four or five different versions, from the King James (in which I, a child of the African Methodist Episcopal Zion Church, had been brought up) to the New English, the International, the Revised Standard, and even the Living Bible.

I wanted to know more than many believed was good for me—a black girlchild destined only to marry and have children and no more in life.

My growing up years were ones split between bursts of athletic energy—as I spent most of my time with the boys in my neighborhood playing every sport available to us as vigorously as I could—and times of reflective quiet spent in bed reading while I recuperated from one illness or another.

Paradoxically, it was those quiet times which always gave me the strength to go back out into the world again. God has always seemed to come to me in days of pain-filled darkness and disillusionment, to hold my hand, to counsel me, to prepare me to go forth renewed in spirit and body.

I left the AME Zion Church at sixteen years of age, against the wishes of my parents, but eventually with their somewhat reluctant acknowledgment (and heartfelt prayer) that I would one day return. I did return to the church in my thirty-second year of life, but it was a different one—the Roman Catholic Church—that opened its arms to me after years of a search I was unaware I had embarked upon.

During those years most of my time was spent in two ways, first furthering my education as I went from high school to college to law school and law practice, then back for further studies on the master's level in environmental science before finding myself working as an attorney for New York State in Albany. Second, it was spent in the mountains and forests of the many state and national parks around the Washington, DC, and Albany areas, with occasional forays overseas.

It was especially on those weekends spent, not in a sterile, stone church, but in the living, spirit-filled wooden cathedrals of God's creation that my faith was constantly reaffirmed and strengthened. I never lost sight of God's "all-powerful hand" during those seventeen years of separation from any institutional form of church; rather, that hand seemed more apparent than ever, leading and guiding me on.

I became a Roman Catholic for one reason only, in response to what I believed then, and still believe today, to be a direct and insistent call from God. It was not a call that initially I wanted to answer because I knew it would totally disrupt the comfortable life I had become accustomed to. But it was a call that I could neither ignore nor deny and still remain the person I thought I was.

To my consternation—and that of my family and friends—I, an independent (some would say "uppity") black woman, found God in the Roman Catholic Church, a church not known particularly for its welcoming attitude toward either blacks or women. Yet I felt nurtured, loved, and desired by God within that church and by the people I was led to who helped me become part of that church, most, but not all, of whom were themselves Roman Catholics.

It is here, during the process of my conversion to Catholicism and my return to graduate school to undertake the study of theology that my life began, for me, to truly reflect the "soul-prayers" expressed in black religious music. For no sooner had I begun the study of the Catholic faith than I was stricken with a degenerative disease in my knees that forced me to leave my beloved woods behind and learn the lesson that God is truly everywhere, supporting us on every leaning side.

The disease, chondromalacia, reduced me, in a few short months, to a pain-filled, grieving, angry woman, bedridden and questioning both her own sanity and that of God. Why become a Catholic if I will never be able to kneel in church, thus making me, as it seemed then at that sensitive stage of conversion, an even more obvious misfit in a parish where there were only four other blacks, a single mother with her three sons?

I wrestled with God on my bed of pain as I do still today. I do not and cannot take God's love simply for granted, but must thrash it out until I can understand, for myself, where I am being led. I argue and shout and listen and pray and question and doubt and finally acquiesce, only to move further down the path to another fork in the road where the struggle begins yet anew.

Since that fateful day in September of 1979 when, while at work, first one, and then the other, knee suddenly swelled up and began to throb unbearably, I have not spent a day of my life without some form of pain, great or small, reminding me of my human frailty and, by extension, of the frailty of others.

Although in time I was able to move beyond braces and crutches to a cane, and eventually to the freedom of walking unassisted once again, I have been made very much aware since that day of God's activity in my own life—an activity which, at times, has seemed paradoxical and unintelligible, but which, over time, has enabled me to take a further step along the path toward home. Over the past fifteen years since my entry into the Roman Catholic Church in 1979, I have undergone major surgery four times, struggled through long periods of recuperation, and, since 1987, dealt with the reality of a chronic illness, rheumatoid arthritis, which I have finally realized and slowly begun to accept will never go away.

Yet during those same fifteen years, I have successfully completed the pontifical program in theology, beginning at the Catholic University of America and finishing with a PhD in religious studies, as well as the Doctor of Sacred Theology (STD) degree from the Catholic University of Louvain in Belgium. I have become an associate, tenured professor at Georgetown University and have discovered the end toward which all of those years of reading had been preparing me: the life of a scholar and teacher, professions equally important to me.

I believe I have learned, because of my own struggles, how to see, hear, and feel the struggles of others, voiced and unvoiced. This has led me to explore theology and the role of the Christian churches in the United States in a new and challenging way—from the bottom up. I know what it is like to be poor, to be discriminated against because of my poverty, my race, my gender, and my disabilities. These many years of struggle and pain, which continue to this day, have forged me in the fiery furnace of God's love. I firmly believe that I have been sent to be of service to those who, unlike myself, have not yet found their voices and been awakened to the graced but burdensome knowledge that, as children of a loving God, they are sent not to suffer, but to live a life free from oppression.

The "soul-prayers" that follow helped carry me over the rock-strewn and rough places of my life over the past years. Although I am, for the most part, referring in them to my ongoing battle with rheumatoid arthritis, in actuality these prayers of my heart reflect all of the years of my journeying toward communion with God—a God whom I know loves and cherishes me.

This story is not over and hopefully will not be over for many years to come. But my growth from anger and despair to acceptance and perseverance is one that I believe is repeated in the lives of many around me who struggle daily with pain, whether its form is physical, mental, or spiritual. And, as I have found, where one form exists, the others are usually close behind.

It is not over. The anger still bubbles to the surface at times; the despair creeps in unannounced and side-swipes me, leaving me befuddled and confused, but the knowledge that through it all God is steadfastly present in my life sustains and strengthens me.

My life, a seeming paradox of contradictions and odd twists and turns, has truly been one where troubles of many different forms have always been in my way. Yet I know now, deep within me, that "trouble don't last always." God is not through with me yet.

YET DO I MARVEL[1]

My life has been a journey of fits and starts, flowing smoothly at times, sluggishly at others, sometimes barely getting anywhere at all, at other times getting "there" much too fast. Part of that journey, especially for the last fifteen years, I have shared with another, the presence of constant pain.

I am a theologian, my head is full of ideas, thoughts, sounds, and words eager to leap forth from my mind through my fingers onto the written page. Yet, the closer I have come to fulfilling what I believe to be my vocation—to be a voice for the voiceless, to be one who stands up for those unable or afraid to stand up for themselves—the more difficult it has become, physically, to do so.

I am a writer whose hands swell up and whose fingers become useless after only a few sentences have been written. Yet I grit my teeth and continue to write, watching the words—so clear and stark in my mind—become scrambled and illegible on the pieces of paper on which I am trying to write.

I am a Roman Catholic who has never knelt in humble submission before the figure of Christ because at the same time that I was in the process of conversion to the Catholic faith, I was also in the process of losing the ability to run, to walk, to stand, and even to kneel. And "yet do I marvel" because, despite all of this, the urge to write, that creative fire, still burns within me, and apparently nothing and no one can quench it. So I have learned to work around and through the pain, rewarding myself with hot baths and heating pads after a certain amount of work has been completed.

I developed rheumatoid arthritis in the last year of my doctoral work at the Catholic University of Louvain in Belgium in 1987. I believe that, although it is thought to be a genetically inherited disease, it was probably also brought on by the stress of completing my dissertation and living in a foreign country with a cold, damp climate. My doctor and I had a running joke as to which would be "finished" first, the dissertation or me, and I almost won (or lost?). The disease did not slowly creep into my life, but burst upon me with a blaze of pain and paralytic fury that only a massive assault of medical treatment could slow down. Even today, when discussing my condition with my new doctor, I feel as if I am describing a war taking place within the confines, the battleground, of my body. We speak of "flare-ups" and "hot-spots," and "assaults" on various joints as if we were anchors on a network news show discussing the latest country under siege. It is a guerrilla war waged by a silent but vicious enemy who has vowed to succeed against all odds, who attacks at odd times, never in the same place, popping out here or there to slow down or stiffen or swell up or immobilize one part or another of my body.

"Yet do I marvel"—for through it all, even despite it all, I still struggle to write, for the voices within me will not be silenced. It is an exhausting battle—I never know from one day to the next whether I will be able to rise to meet the dawn or will have to greet it lying flat on my back or sitting up somewhere in between. Making plans can become meaningless and frustrating when the legs you believed would carry you out for a walk on a sunny day decide they would prefer not to carry any weight at all today—thank you anyway.

It is frustrating, yet I do not—I cannot—give up. The struggle is within me and all around me, yet still I fight to put the words down that speak to me and, hopefully, to others— words of freedom, of liberation, of faith in a God who loves, a God who frees, a God who "makes a way out of no way."

There are times when I do not understand why I have this disease. There are times when I feel like giving up—giving in to the pain and simply letting it take over not just my body, but my mind as well. Yet I find I cannot do that. For I am constantly and persistently called out of myself by those around me who seem to feel that my words bring hope into their lives. They do not realize how much their response brings hope back into mine. And so I marvel at this curious thing, "that God would make a poet black, and bid [her] sing!" I, a black woman, at times completely overpowered by this disease that has taken up residence within me, am bidden over and over by this God, in whom I have put all of my trust, to sing.

And so I sing, and in the singing I too am free. So I share with you the prayers of my soul not in bitterness or in defeat, but in acknowledgment of the importance of prayer and God's love in my life. I also hope that my words, written in and about suffering, may ease your own.

Most of these pieces were written during the time from dusk to dawn when, because of pain or malaise caused by my disease or due to the effects of the many different medicines I take to curb it, I was unable to sleep. Many times I found peace in those still hushed hours; at other times, only anger and frustration. All of these feelings fueled this collection of essays I

have entitled "soul prayers" because I do believe that they come
from the very depths of my soul.

I KNOW WHAT THE CAGED BIRD FEELS

Sympathy[2]

I know what the caged bird feels, alas!
When the sun is bright on the upland slopes;
When the wind stirs soft through the springing grass
And the river flows like a stream of glass;
When the first bird sings and the first bud opes,
And the faint perfume from its chalice steals—
I know what the caged bird feels!
I know why the caged bird beats his wing
Till its blood is red on the cruel bars:
For he must fly back to his perch and cling
When he fain would be on the bough a-swing:
And a pain still throbs in the old, old scars
And they pulse again with a keener sting—
I know why he beats his wing!
I know why the caged bird sings, ah me,
When his wing is bruised and his bosom sore—
When he beats his bars and would be free;
It is not a carol of joy or glee,
But a prayer that he sends from his heart's deep core,
But a plea, that upward to Heaven he flings—
I know why the caged bird sings!

—Paul Laurence Dunbar

Yes, "I know what the caged bird feels." The words of Paul
Laurence Dunbar's poignant poem sound in my ears and in the
corners of my mind almost constantly now. Truly, "I know

what the caged bird feels, alas!" At first, when I was told that the reason for my strange aches and pains, for the stiffness in my hands and knees, was rheumatoid arthritis, I simply took it in stride, or so I thought. Another battle to overcome. My life, it seems, has been plagued (or, perhaps, blessed) with various battles that had to be fought one by one. As a black woman in the United States, I am used to fighting battles. But this one was different.

I could not ignore it, because if I did I found myself slowly freezing into an immovable statue. I could not bargain with it: "Okay, I'll stay in bed all of today but tomorrow I'm going hiking." This disease was sneaky; it did not—and still does not—play fair. It is insidious and pervasive; it has infiltrated every part of my being, every one of my joints, clamoring for attention, seeking to be heard and dealt with. It is not willing to be put aside until I am able to deal with it in my own time. It has a rhythm of its own which, as yet, I cannot accustom myself to.

I cannot run away from it because I can no longer run. In the past five years since rheumatoid arthritis began its pernicious assault on my body, I have become a shadow of the person I was. Once a year-round athlete, proficient in too many sports to name and loving the strength and vigor of my body, now I find myself exhausted after a two-block walk, unable to keep up with my own mother who is almost thirty years older than I. I am confined, restrained by the body that once took me everywhere and with which I did so much. I am now its captive rather than its master.

And so I mourn like the caged bird at the change of seasons, at the coming of spring when I would be the first on the hills seeking out the new-budding azaleas and rhododendrons. I grieve over the fall with its flamboyant burst of colors running riot in woods where I no longer can easily walk. I wander lost through the winters and springs without my usual bearings, my senses heightened but my responses dulled.

But as I grieve, I cannot help thinking of others who are also trapped, not like myself in a cage made by the body, but in the cages made by others—the cages of the ghettos and barrios, the barred rooms of poverty and the locked doors of despair. And I wonder. I wonder why I have been afflicted in this way. Is it not burden enough, at times, to be both black and female? Why have others, like myself, been afflicted with poverty or illness or illiteracy?

Is it the will of God? No, for my God is a good and loving God who does not inflict pain and suffering for the hell of it. Is it my fault? No, for I, and these others, have committed no sin or evil for which we should be punished. God does not punish; he[3] is a God of forgiveness and freedom. It is not a crime to be poor or homeless or black or a woman. The blame, if blame there is, must be laid at the doors of a society that finds fault with those seen as "handicapped" because of their race, gender, age, or physical condition. However, those of us so "afflicted" are left with the responsibility, the necessity, of overcoming the limitations—whether real or imposed—that we face, and of working, as best we can, to become the persons we are capable of being, by overcoming the pain, by obtaining the skills necessary to rise out of poverty, by taking charge of our own lives, by allowing no one to "turn us around." And it is God, my faith in him, our faith in him that gives the strength and the courage to do so.

And "I know why the caged bird sings." Hers is a song of a free spirit trapped against its will, of a being meant for the vastness of the sky but pinned down and trapped in a space so small that sometimes breath itself seems impossible. And what breath there is, is spent screaming (singing?) out frustration, rage, fear, and, hopefully, in the midst of it all, the determination to ''make it over.''

I see myself growing slower, stiffer, pain-bound, and illness-ridden, and I see so many others—young of body and strong of heart—who are also prevented by lack of opportunity, by the sins of racism and sexism and all other "-isms," from living as they choose, from being the person they would like to be and are capable of being. And I recognize my calling. It is a calling, a vocation, a request from God. It is a calling to serve others, to learn from my pain and my frustration, to be able to share it with others who also feel trapped (but whose bars are less visible than my own because they have been artificially created and imposed) so that they will realize that they are not alone. I think of women imprisoned for their gender, men and women trapped by others' view of their race, the elderly tossed aside in barren and abusive homes, and so many others captive through no fault of their own. As my body weakens, my mind grows ever sharper, honed to slice away at the useless and the nonsensical and to do the only thing I can do, "speak the truth," as poet Mari Evans proclaims. I must speak the truth that human beings are not meant to be caged, but to be free, whether black, brown, red, yellow, or white, every color of the rainbow. Whether physically or mentally handicapped, whether male or female, we are all God's creation and are meant to be free. But that freedom must come not only from without; that will come in time. It must first come from within, from the very core of our beings, from the very depths of our soul.

It is not enough to beat against the bars that encircle me, bars made up of my very flesh and bone, because I cannot change them. I cannot free myself in that sense. But I can free myself through my spirit that cannot be vanquished. I can free myself with the power of my words, flying high above and away from my no longer functioning body. Strengthened in spirit, I can serve to free others from the artificial cages in which they have been placed because of their race, their sex, their poverty, their age, or the language they speak or are unable to speak. My words can serve as hammers to beat open the doors so that they can begin their own journey, their own flight of freedom.

It is with my song, with my words, that I break down the barriers that separate me from you. It is the ultimate irony: I, who am a prisoner of my own body, can be a key to open the locked doors of the minds and hearts of others.

Yes, "I know what the caged bird feels, alas!" And I know why it beats its captive wings until they bleed bright drops of blood because I still rage against this crippling disease that has so quickly and quietly made me its captive. But I also "know why the caged bird sings." And I shall continue to sing my song of freedom. I shall fling my prayer of hope for all who are captive against their will, against the very gates of heaven, until I am called home "to be with God." By serving others, I am serving myself and my God; by seeking the liberation of all who are oppressed, I know I shall one day too be free.

LET GO AND LET GOD

The mothers of the black church, those elderly women who have worked hard all of their lives, often with so little reward, have a way of saying, whenever something goes wrong or someone is burdened more than they feel they can bear, "You just have to 'let go and let God.'" As a child, I would look at these strong black women who I knew had been through so much in their lives, and who were still going through difficult times, and wonder what they meant. What did it mean to "let go and let God"? Let go of what, or was it who? Was it a person, place, or a thing that was supposed to be "let go" of? And what did God have to do with it? Let God what? Do something, say something, be something? It seemed an unanswerable question, a statement lost in the mystery of greater age and wisdom than mine. I must admit I often felt impatient or annoyed when I was advised to "let go and let God, child" because I could not figure out how—or perhaps did not have the patience or faith—to turn my troubles over to a God I was not completely sure of.

Over the years of my growing up, both in and out of the black church, but always within the black community that was its foundation, I slowly began to understand what those old women, who in my mind had seen and experienced it all, meant. They had experienced both the joys and the sorrows that human life has to bring. Yet, they could, when necessary, simply "let go and let God."

They could "let go" of the pain of losing a child through illness or misfortune or of watching another child or their husband slowly give up hope of getting a meaningful job, of having something tangible to produce at day's end. They could "let go" of the racism that connfronted them at every turn, of being called out of their rightful name and having to respond humbly to those who were less God-fearing than themselves, and they could "let God" carry those sorrows for a while. God did not take over the pain, the frustration, or the anger—it was still there—but they could rest their burden with the Lord for just a little while until they found the strength to take it up and carry it again. Some would say they were passive, that the older generation did not "let God," but "let racists" step on them while they found refuge in a spiritual realm. But they would be wrong. Some fail to see the strength and courage that "letting go" provided these women—strength and courage that enabled them to, yes, sometimes turn the other cheek, but also to keep fighting for better times for their children and their children's children. They were not fighting for themselves but for those coming down the line.

Today, as I battle with my own fears and doubts, my own frustrations (about who I am and where I am going) and yearnings for a life free from pain, free from prejudice and discrimination, free from the constant struggle to survive and simply be me, I have come to realize that there are times when life becomes infinitely more tolerable if the burden is shared, with human friends, yes, but even more important, shared with a God who loves and watches over me like a "mother hen brooding over her chicks." It is that same God who has said, "Behold, while you were in your mother's womb, I knew you and I named you. How could I love you less now?"

To "let go and let God" is to put yourself into the hands of God, even for just a little while, until the challenges of life are more bearable. It enables us to step away from the seeming chaos of today's world and to be at peace for a time while we catch our breath. By "letting go" of our earthly cares from time to time, it is so much easier to "let God" help us manage them when once again we are confronted with them and must take them upon our shoulders. It is not a form of "otherworldly" escape, for the pain, the anger, the fears, the frustrations are always, sadly, a part of life, not because God wants it so, but because of our own human failure to make it different.

My God is a "wonder-working God" who shares the burdens of this world with me and, in so doing, helps me to learn of both my strengths and my weaknesses. This strong and loving God reveals to me the way I need to be for those around me—a nurturer, a healer, a sustainer, and a friend.

Powerful and loving God
Walk with me this day
*   for just a little while,*
For my body grows weary
*   and my feet falter and stumble.*

I feel overwhelmed by the pressures
    of my life, the demands of family, career, health,
    society; all the many things that seem so important and
    yet are not always as important as I think.
I lift up my hands and heart to you in faith
    knowing that when I can no longer carry on
You will be there to carry me onward.
Help me to accept my limitations
    and to acknowledge my weaknesses.
Help me to recognize my strengths and to use
    them in ways that are healing and holy for others.
Help me to "let go" of my problems and concerns
    and to "let" you be "God.

I DON'T FEEL NO WAYS TIRED

I don't feel no ways tired,
I come too far from where I started from,
Nobody told me that the road would be easy,
I don't believe He brought me this far to leave me.[4]

Liberation comes in all shapes and forms. There is the physical release from pain that comes in death—quick and sudden or slow and tedious, but release eventually comes and one can "go home and be with God."

Then there is the liberation that comes from a deeply held faith in a God who saves, a "wonder-working" God, a God who can make everything all right, who frees us from the many pains and problems of the day and enables us to go on about our business of helping to bring about the coming of the Kingdom.

There is the liberation of sharing one's life with another, of being able to "let go" at times, knowing the one with whom you have pledged to live and share your future will step in and hold on for a while and that, in turn, you can and will do the same for him or her.

There is liberation in death; there is liberation in faith; there is liberation in love. There is also liberation in struggling to make a positive difference in the lives of others, even when your own seems to be "going to hell in a handbasket." I do not mean a life of martyrdom or extreme sacrifice, simply a life of being lovingly present to others when they are seeking answers, when they are trying to "make it over" into the Kingdom, when they are seeking the right way to go and need guidance in choosing their next steps, need a listening ear and a caring heart even when you, yourself, are so tired and weary that each step seems like an uphill climb.

It is freeing—a painful freedom perhaps—to realize that God can and does speak through you even at times when you feel God is farthest away from you.

My life has been so difficult of late that I have felt isolated and apart from God. The old friendly camaraderie and kinship I used to feel has disappeared and nothing seems to be rushing in to take its place. There is an emptiness within me that once was filled, a hollowness that once was solid, a yearning that once was fulfilled. And I mourn the loss from within that emptiness, within that hollowness, within that yearning.

At times I feel deserted by God, left alone in this harsh world to struggle with my now clumsy and blinded body toward the light that once shined so brightly. But then I am asked to speak to others of what I have learned in my seemingly slow and painful journey toward Christ, and something miraculous happens. Words come, words that somehow seem to lift people's hearts, words that lighten their burdens and give them the relief of tears, words that give them hope and wonder, and I realize that God is still here, within me, giving me voice.

The emptiness, the hollowness, the yearning I feel is caused, I realize, by my own inability to accept and acknowledge the new me that is being built out of the fragmented mold of the person I once was. I am no longer whole; I am no longer able. I lean upon the Lord and others because I must, and I hate that because it demeans the image I have of myself as a free and independent being.

Yet I realize, as I see and feel the reactions of those around me when I speak words inspired by God alone, that I am still free, I am still independent. But it is a new freedom, a new independence, a freeing of myself to be used by God as an instrument, as a sounding board—but not a passive one. No! For I struggle and fight and yell and scream against that usage, yet when it happens, oh, the peace, the liberating, restful peace that flows throughout me and revives my soul again. And I wonder at my fears and my angers and, most especially, at my self-doubt, my feelings of unworthiness at being used in this way.

It is exhausting, It is wearing me out, this constant struggle. I want to hear God's voice directly within me as once I used to, a voice that guided and sustained me in my journey. I want God to talk to me, not through me. Yet, when I stop struggling and fighting, I realize that I am simply moving one step farther on my own journey and one step closer to that promised liberation, when all of humanity is truly made one. My prayer, then, is to use me, Lord, again and again if it means others will not suffer, others will have their hopes renewed, their faith enriched. And I begin to hear once again those words that have sustained me throughout the years of my journeying toward God:

> *I don't feel no ways tired.*
> *I come too far from where I started from,*
> *Nobody told me that the road would be easy,*
> *I don't believe He brought me this far to leave me.*

I do feel tired at times, but the tiredness is only physical and it soon lifts, for I realize that the road I have chosen is one to which I have been guided from afar. Although at times I feel forsaken and alone, I know God is still guiding me, for life has brought me a "mighty long way." God has faith in me even when, especially when, I have no faith of my own.

NOTES

1. The title is from the poem of the same name by Countee Cullen, Harlem Renaissance poet. Countee Cullen, "Yet Do I Marvel," *My Soul's High Song: The Collected Writings of Countee Cullen* (New York: Anchor Books, 1991), 79.

2. *The Poetry of Black America: An Anthology of the 20th Century,* ed. Arnold Adolf (New York and San Francisco: Harper & Row), 8.

3. Throughout this text, I use "he" for God. This is because, for me, God has always been male, not in any patriarchal or oppressive sense, but in the sense of God as loving father and caring brother. I also see God as female and as spirit (without gender). But in these soul prayers, I am speaking to, with, and about God in my own understanding. The reader is free to use whatever language about God he or she prefers.

4. Lyrics by Curtis Burrell.

5

Were You There?

Stations of the Cross

STATION IV
Jesus Meets His Mother

This is my son. My son, with thorns piercing his tender flesh, the blood running down his face. He is so young, so handsome. He is my son, my child. I remember so clearly when the angel came to tell me I was to bear a child, a son who would be great among his people. I was overwhelmed. I knew not what to think or say. What would people think? I was betrothed but had never been with a man. How could this be? What would happen to me, to this child? But I knew I would say yes. I was called to this by God, and I trusted in God. So I said yes.

But is this what the angel meant by greatness? What could come of such pain, such indignity? This is my child. I would carry the cross for him as once I carried him, laughing and crying, on my back. What greatness can come at such a fearful price?

How long, how long, O Lord, must we mothers watch in silent agony as our children die before their time, weighed

---

First published in Diana L. Hayes, *Were You There? Stations of the Cross* (Maryknoll, NY: Orbis Books, 2000), 49–54. Verses are from the Spirituals.

down by so many needless crosses not of their own making? Crosses of skin color, of poverty, of language, of sexual orientation, of fear, of lost hopes and discarded dreams. How long, O Lord, how long?

We cannot remain silent. These are our children, whether they came from our wombs or the wombs of others, helpless infants needing love and care. And now they die, at each other's hands, at the hands of those who were meant to care for them, the hands of indifference, of anger, of a corrosive hatred. These are our children, no matter how old or how young. They die. They die senselessly, needlessly, blindly, unknowing, without understanding why they must pay such a price. How long, O Lord, how long will this senseless slaughter continue?

Truly a sword is piercing my heart, the pain is so great. How could this be happening to my child, to my son? I remember when he was born. The night was so clear and the stars so bright they seemed to come right into that old stable where we had taken shelter. The warmth of the animals surrounded us as my labor began. I was so worried; this was my first and I had no one to help me. Elizabeth, my cousin, and the other women were back in Nazareth as I lay, racked with pain, in Bethlehem, the place of my husband's family. I had feared the ride on the donkey would cause my time to come, as the older women of the village had warned me. But we had no choice; we had to return to Bethlehem for the census.

And now my time had come. My little one was so eager to come forth I could barely control him. My husband tried to help but he was just a man, overwhelmed by the miracle of new life. The animals seemed to stare in wonder. Perhaps they knew what I was going through to bring forth this new life, a new life with so much promise. All mothers believe the same. How can they not? Each child is precious, an individual miracle, with a full life ahead. It was happening so quickly. He was born, my son, my little Jesus.

The Virgin Mary had a baby boy.
The Virgin Mary had a baby boy.
The Virgin Mary had a baby boy.
And they gave him the name of Jesus.

Jesus looks at me now as he has done so many times since he first looked at me in the stable. His big brown eyes seem to be full of the pain of the world. Who is this man, my child, my son? I hardly know him any more, he has changed so. I was so proud of him as he gathered his followers and so many came forward to join him. He preached with such beauty and faith. This is my child, but truly he is God's as well. I thought I knew him, but every moment seems to reveal him in so many different ways.

The cross is so large. It seems to bear the weight of the world. Why is my son walking to his death dragging this heavy wooden cross? What has he done? He is so young and innocent. He has simply tried to do what God called him to do, to proclaim a message of peace and love for all of humankind. Why do so many see him and his message as a threat when it is a promise of unparalleled joy? He was not the first to speak God's word, but when he spoke, I saw entire crowds transformed, their faces, narrow with the pain of poverty and injustice, lighting up with a hope they had never before felt. All to whom he spoke, whom he touched, were transformed as I had been. His very presence spoke as much as his actions.

And now he walks to his death, but somehow I know, deep within myself, that his life will not end like that of others. There is more to come. His birth, witnessed by stable animals, peasants, and those three men from afar with their incredible gifts, his life, so brief, his death—all herald the coming glory of God. Truly I am blessed among all women to have been given the grace of being the mother of such a one, to have carried him within me for nine months, to have brought him forth in such pain and happiness. But for what? At times, his actions have brought me such fear, such pain. What is to become of my child? He is so young to die such a painful death. But I look at him and see his strength and resolve, and I am calmed. I fear for him because I am his mother but, like all mothers, I must let him go. His journey began with me, but now we come to a parting of our ways. His destiny calls him, and he walks on bent under that cross of wood. I send him on his way with a mother's blessing, with my love to sustain him, for it is all I have to give.

> *He come from the Kingdom.*
> *He come from the glorious Kingdom!*

Jesus was a strong man, a man sent to carry the burdens of the world upon his shoulders, transforming them into the joys of salvation. Where are the strong men of today? Where are our sons and their fathers? So many are bowed down and beaten or fighting the wrong enemies, or each other, rather than the poverty, hatred, and ignorance that keeps them trapped in meaningless lives of little hope.

Where are our strong young men, young men like Jesus, who stepped forward to fight the good fight, not just for themselves but for all who are wrongly used, imprisoned, struck down in the fullness of life? Where are our men of God like Martin, Malcolm, and Medgar, who walked this earth such a short time ago?

Their mothers seek them. Their children wait for them, with empty bellies and even emptier hearts. What has happened to our young men that has caused them to give up, succumbing to the temptations of this world, giving us their very souls little by little by little until there's nothing left to give?

Our faith no longer sustains them. The churches are empty, except for the old and the very young. The children are in the streets, filled with anger at the betrayal of the promise given to them at birth, the promise of a future filled with possibilities. They are burdened with new crosses that imprison rather than free them, crosses of crack cocaine, HIV/AIDS, death at the hands of strangers and of friends, children whom they have no time for or interest in, jobs that provide money to sustain them but give no joy, lives of emptiness but crammed with busyness.

We must reclaim these, our wayward children. We must gather them to ourselves and listen to their fears and their pain. We must meet them, as Mary did, on their painful journeys and attempt, through word and touch, to help them to see that they are not alone. We, their mothers, are with them; we will not abandon them, and neither will Jesus because he knows their sorrow and is acquainted with their grief. He is one of us and walks with us regardless of who we are and what we have done or failed to do. We wring our hands, feeling the pain of our young men as they wander like ghosts in a nightmare, but we also turn and walk alongside them, letting them know by our presence that they have not been and will not be abandoned. We are their mothers and we are not ashamed of their condition. We are their mothers and they are still our children. We must reclaim them, for they too come from the kingdom, that glorious kingdom of God.

STATION VI
Veronica Wipes the Face of Jesus

Beautiful, also, are the souls of my Black sisters.

—Langston Hughes

Black women have carried a double and oftentimes triple burden in this world, for they are black, female, and too often poor in a world that disparages all three. Bowed down by ignorance, usually willful, and misunderstanding, they have, far too often, been required to carry the weight of the world on their weary shoulders.

Since the beginning of time, they have, as women, been blamed for the entry of evil into the world. The stereotypes that plague their every step—of overbearing matriarch, emasculating wife, and oversexed seductress—have followed them like a curse from generation to generation. Yet, somehow, they persevere.

I heard my mother say,
I heard my mother say,
I heard my mother say,
Give me Jesus.

In the face of seemingly insurmountable odds, they are able to keep their faith alive as they attempt—despite rejection and the loss of husbands, brothers, fathers, and sons—to nurture that faith and pass it along to those of their own time and to those of coming after them. They forge a chain of faith that passes down through the centuries, over rivers, valleys, and oceans.

Give me Jesus, Give me Jesus,
You may have all this world,
Give me Jesus.

They stand firm, refusing to back down in the face of danger, assaults against themselves and, more important, against theirs, to encounter their child, their son, Jesus. Their hearts cry out at the pain they see furrowing his forehead, and one, Veronica, attempts to wipe it away with a piece of cloth. The soldiers are caught off guard and don't know how to respond; looks of consternation cross their faces. But Jesus, still being helped by Simon, pauses, looks at them, and blesses their faith and kindness. They too have gained salvation because they did not hesitate to comfort the Comforter in his time of need.

Veronica, unaware, receives a further blessing: the image of Jesus' face on her cloth as a sign of her faithfulness. So many women today remain unknown, faceless and forgotten, despite the courageous and countless acts of mercy they have performed down through the years. The unknown black slave woman who knew the alphabet and a little bit of reading, knowledge that could have led to her death if discovered, who held classes at night after a hard day in the fields and taught class after class. Many took their new knowledge, forged passes, and fled, but she stayed behind, providing a way to the future. The women who sewed quilts, today seen as valuable pieces of folk art but then only as scraps sewn together to keep warm. The pattern on these quilts also provided guidance regarding the path to the North and freedom.

> *Dark midnight was my cry,*
> *Dark midnight was my cry,*
> *Dark midnight was my cry,*
> *Give me Jesus.*

There were women then of strength and an enduring courage, and those women still exist today, countless numbers of women who serve, unnamed and unknown, in homes, hot kitchens, shelters, hospices, schools, and churches, cooking, sewing, and cleaning, teaching and preaching a way out of no way into God's graced freedom.

> *Give me Jesus,*
> *Give me Jesus,*
> *You may have all of this world,*
> *Give me Jesus.*

Veronica and the women with her boldly walked up to Jesus, ignoring the soldiers and their weapons, and offered him aid. They prayed for him, giving him strength, their strength, to continue his journey, as mothers have prayed for their children for countless generations. Today other women walk with their children, of every nation and tongue, with their sons in jail, in school, or in corporate or political office, with their daughters college-bound or pregnant at too young an age. They walk because they must, because they love, because they care. They reveal the inner strength of women. They reveal the courage of women. They reveal the faith of women.

Oh, when I come to die,
Oh, when I come to die,
Oh, when I come to die,
Give me Jesus.

Give me Jesus,
Give me Jesus,
You may have all of this world,
Give me Jesus.

STATION VIII
Jesus Meets the Women of Jerusalem

They were women then
My mama's generation
Husky of voice—stout of step
With fists as well as hands
How they battered down doors...

—Alice Walker

The women of Jerusalem gathered by the side of the path they knew Jesus would take. They greeted him with cries of pain and love. The One whom they loved was being taken from them. They stood in the path, knelt in the dirt, and stormed the heavens with their pain-filled wailing.

Jesus, his brow streaming with blood and salty sweat, his robe sodden and soggy with the same awful mix, hears them and recovers his strength to stand. He looks at the women who had followed him, who had believed in him, and who continued to do so, and was overcome.

The soldiers are dumbstruck. They know not how to counter these women, their women, their wives and mothers, sisters and daughters kneeling in the dust with their crying children at their side and praising, through their tears, this man whom they are taking to his death. Why are the women showing him such respect? He is no better than a common slave or thief, to be hung between two other thieves, the worst death possible. Who was this man that many have condemned and yet so many others have exalted?

The women knew the truth of him. They understood the significance of his life and death; they cried but also rejoiced that they were able to see him, to strengthen him on his way. They knew him as he knew them.

They knew what Jesus had told them, that the future was bleak and their lives and their children's lives would be as nothing to those who were capable of killing such a man.

> Daughters of Jerusalem, do not weep for me; weep instead for yourselves and for your children, for indeed, the days are coming when people will say, "Blessed are the barren, the wombs that never bore and the breasts that never nursed." (Luke 23:28–29)

Harsh words, indeed, from one about to die but, in their hearts, they knew the truth of his words. And many lived to see them come to pass with the destruction of the temple and the scattering of their people.

Today, we, too, can see the truth of Jesus' words. Look at our cities, our schools, our streets and the devastation and despair present there. Look also at our children, of every tongue and nation. They are old before their time, forced to take on duties and responsibilities beyond their years. They are confronted with choices no one should have, child or adult. Should they become gang members, to find the family that no longer exists at home or to provide themselves with protection from others? Should they try drugs, which are available on every street corner, even in their schoolyards, or listen to their parents and other adults who warn them of the dangers while they themselves are smoking and drinking themselves to death?

It is not easy being a child today. Children look for certitude, for guidance from the adults around them, but too often find themselves their victims instead. We fill our lives with so many important things that we have no time for life, for the children, for their hopes and dreams. They grow bitter and angry, foulmouthed and profane. They laugh off school as a waste of time or pursue an education with a single-mindedness that leaves no room for the simple pleasures of life. They have too many role models who refuse to act as such and too few who are capable of helping them to make the right decisions in their lives.

Our children, bereft of all that sustains and nurtures life, find themselves too often abandoned and alone. And the women, the mothers, cry. They cry for Jesus; they cry for themselves; they cry for their children and the loss of hope.

Women bear the future in their wombs. They are the bearers of culture, the tellers of stories, the weavers of dreams. They, too, have fallen victim, like so many men, to the easy way out, the quick climb up the ladder of success, abandoning all they believed in along the way, or the even quicker fall into substance abuse and prostitution for the quick release from pain, fear, and frustration.

Jesus walks on to his destiny knowing that it will end in glory, the salvation of us all. We walk on as well, some quickly and surely, others stumbling and faltering, all, all seeking the Way, the true path of life.

> *Amazing grace*
> *How sweet the sound*
> *That saved a wretch like me*
> *I once was lost*
> *But now am found,*
> *Was blind but now I see.*

Open your eyes. See the world around us, crumbling into chaos. Draw strength from the One who gave His life so that all might live. And live!

STATION XIV
Jesus Is Laid in the Tomb

Were you there when they laid him in the tomb?

It is finished. The crowd begins to move away. The man Jesus is dead. He has been wrapped in cloth, just as he was wrapped at his birth in the cold stable, and carried to the tomb. There are no shepherds sent by angels, no wise men come to honor him. Just his mother and a few courageous friends. His mother, Mary, walks alongside Jesus as he is carried to the tomb where he will be laid. Her head is bowed, her hands held together in prayer. "Thy will, not mine, O Lord," the words her son uttered in humble submission in the garden.

Were you there when they laid him in the tomb?

Now it is over. The dream has died with this gentle man of humble origins. He was a carpenter and a fisher of men and women who dared to preach God's love for the least among us, the poor, the widowed and orphaned, the women, those beaten down by despair and disease.

The women had remained faithful in the face of the threat of arrest and condemnation. They prayed, standing at his feet as he hung dying. They helped to bring him down from the cross and gave him to his mother to be cradled one last time in her arms. They wept with her and walked with him to his place of rest.

Had the dream died? Was this the end of it all? Jesus, the man, was dead. His lifeless body lay in the tomb waiting for the stone to be rolled across the front, sealing him and the hopes of so many inside.

Were you there when they laid him in the tomb?

The events of that day were so incredible that many still could not believe what they had seen and heard. When this man died, the earth shuddered as if in labor, the sky suddenly grew as dark as night in the middle of the day. Even the soldiers, boldly gambling over his clothing, were shaken, their leader exclaiming the first words of Christian faith: Surely, this man was the Son of God.

Oh, sometimes it causes me to tremble, tremble, tremble.

The earth trembled; the saints rose and walked the earth; the hearts of the hardest were opened. The veil of the temple was torn in two, and darkness—a great darkness as if all creation was in mourning—engulfed the sky.

This man, Jesus, in his few years on earth preaching the Good News of God, had an impact unlike any man before him. He had lived a life of poverty, working with his hands. His followers had been, for the most part, humble men and women—fishermen, tax collectors, prostitutes, the sick, the lepers, the poor, slaves. For them, his words had opened up new possibilities in life, a life not of constant, endless, thankless, drudgery, but a new life, one of plenty and peace, of a new freedom of mind, body, and spirit.

Were you there when they laid him in the tomb?

How could this be? It was now finished. Had it all been a dream? The miraculous events of the past were forgotten and those to come not known as yet. As poor in death as in life, Jesus was laid in a tomb belonging to Joseph of Arimathea, a wealthy man who had earlier engaged Jesus in debate and found his life completely changed. He donated his own newly carved tomb, hewn out of the very rocks of the mountain where Jesus had been crucified.

How is it possible for life to go on after one you loved perhaps more than life itself is now dead? How do we keep from sinking into despair and hopeless grief? How do we maintain our faith, knowing that the one we loved no longer walks the earth alongside us? How? How?

We go on because we know the rest of the story. We know that Jesus' death is not the end, either of his life or of ours. His death is a new beginning, one unattainable before. By his death and glorious resurrection, death itself has been conquered and is no longer a threat to us.

Glory! Alleluia!

Jesus' death on the cross, his burial in the tomb, teaches us that death is not the end. After death comes a new life, one without pain or suffering, without fear or doubt, a life of joy that goes beyond all human understanding.

> *Why should I feel discouraged?*
> *Why should the shadows come?*
> *Why should my heart be lonely?*
> *And long for heaven and home?*

> *When Jesus is my portion,*
> *My constant friend is he.*
> *His eye is on the sparrow*
> *And I know he watches me.*

Regardless of the pain we feel at the loss of a loved one, regardless of the anger and fear when someone betrays a trust, we must remember that God does indeed watch over us all. Things are not what they seem. The faithful will always overcome any and all obstacles in their paths in the end. Why? Because God, our Creator, promised it would be so, and Jesus, our Savior, died so that it would be so. Death is not an ending but a beginning. The cross does not stand for suffering and pain but for life, a life in Christ sustained by a deep and steadfast faith, a faith that "moves mountains" and turns the darkest of days into a day of rejoicing.

> *I sing because I'm happy.*
> *I sing because I'm free.*
> *For his eye is on the sparrow*
> *And I know he watches me.*

He watches me and you. All of God's creation is under God's loving care. For we have been promised the same victory over death that Christ was promised as long as we believe and persevere in our faith.

It is this faith that enabled our ancestors to withstand the long, hot days of cruel, seemingly endless labor. It is this faith that brought so many to these shores to begin a new life and enabled them to rebuild those lives after years of war, poverty, tragedy, poor education, and despair. It is this faith that caused our brothers and sisters in Christ to dance and sing of their joy and love of Jesus Christ.

They were indeed happy and so indeed should we be if we share that same faith in a wonder-working God, a take-charge God, a righteous God, a liberating God, a God who makes a way out of no way.

> *Nobody knows the trouble I've seen,*
> *Nobody knows my sorrow.*
> *Nobody knows the trouble I've seen,*
> *Glory! Alleluia!*

How did they do it? How could they sing of trouble that is unparalleled and pervasive yet conclude with praise and thanksgiving? How, but through faith, an undying, unbeatable faith? Jesus died on the cross and was laid to rest in a donated tomb. His followers walked away in grief and sorrow.

But we know the rest of the story! We know that Jesus rose again on the third day, that the stone was rolled away and that he walked out in resurrected glory. Glory! Alleluia! He went before those who continued to believe in him into Galilee, where he commissioned them to spread the Good News of God's coming throughout the world for all of time. He then returned to his Father as we too shall one day return to the Father and Mother of us all.

> *Glory! Alleluia!*

Turn away from fear. Turn away from anger and violence. Look for and find the face of Jesus shining out of each and every person that you meet, whoever and wherever they may be. Like you, they too are struggling with their faith. Believe in Jesus and be fulfilled! He is not dead! There is joy, great joy, to come if we only believe and live our lives in accordance with that belief.

Glory! Alleluia!

6

Who Do You, God, Say That We Are?

Where are we going? Why do we act in the ways that we do? Where will it all end? Is there a purpose, a reason for our existence, or is life simply happenstance? Despite the negative prophecies by scientists of the nineteenth and twentieth centuries, religion persists, and human beings still ask questions that science has been unable to answer about their own existence and the world around them. In the last century most of the questions have dealt with the issue of "who God is for us" as human beings. How do we see God and God's actions in our lives? Is God still actively engaged in human history or has God retreated to the heavens, observing with a cold and austere eye our fumbling attempts at becoming like gods ourselves?

We have been so busy asking who God is for us that we have forgotten that we were made for God, not God for us. God cannot be captured in a box, in a church, mosque, temple, or synagogue, nor in a piece of music, a prayer, rite, or ritual. God is in all of these, and so much more. We cannot control God's being by defining or describing it, any more than God seeks to control

---

Originally published in Mary Hembrow Snyder, ed., *Spiritual Questions for the Twenty-First Century: Essays in Honor of Joan D. Chittister* (Maryknoll, NY: Orbis Books, 2001), 53–56.

ours. But in our haste to get ahead we have lost sight of the fullness of our freedom, boxing ourselves into narrow concepts and understandings of both God and humanity. We think we have captured God's essence, as well as our own, only to discover in time that we have captured nothing but ourselves.

Is this the question for the next century, that asked by Jesus of Peter: "Who do you say that I am?" I would argue that the question has changed. Unlike the people of the first century or even of the eighteenth, we are no longer in touch with ourselves, with our humanity, with our creatureliness as beings created by a loving God. We have, for the most part, lost contact with our inner selves, which have been psychoanalyzed into a quivering mass of naked psychoses.

To be a spirit-filled person, one with an intimate relationship with an all-powerful, all-loving Being beyond human finitude has come to be seen as a fault or failure, something to be scorned and rejected, analyzed, examined, and eradicated as a weakness. The freedom and beauty of a spiritual life, closely connected with and inseparable from one's everyday life, has been twisted and turned into a neatly defined package of teachings, beliefs, and acts that must be adhered to at all costs. Anyone whose expression of the spirit does not conform to this neatly wrapped box is seen as heretical or psychically immature.

Faith in something or someone greater than oneself is suspect in today's business-oriented, individualistic world. It is seen as a harmful dependency. Yet peoples throughout the world, especially in the highly industrialized nations, find themselves at a loss, seeking after something or someone, or some meaning in their lives that they cannot even name. There is an emptiness within them that all of the busyness of their overscheduled and highly organized lives cannot seem to fill. That yearning is not being answered by our churches, our synagogues, or any of the other traditional forms of institutional religion. Perhaps this is so because these institutions have become so involved in naming and thereby controlling the Spirit that they no longer have it within their midst. Once the arbiters of social, cultural, moral, and even political mores, they are increasingly seen as enclaves of the elite or as moral policemen, sites of condemnation and judgment rather than of welcome and affirmation. The roles once seen as their preserve have been taken over by other, private and public organizations without any religious affiliation. They have lost that which they sought and claimed to own and have become "whitened sepulchers" devoid of life, of knowledge, of hope, of the spirit.

Many people have turned to other sources, religious and otherwise, seeking to satisfy their hunger for meaning. All the while, they seem unable to comprehend that the answer lies within themselves and those around them. For the answer to their eternal questions of self and belonging, the answer to the paramount question for this age, "Who am I and why?" can only be God in God's self and as God is reflected in the faces of all our fellow human beings. For we have truly lost our own way in the world. We have turned against each other, refusing to acknowledge the Other's humanity and godliness because today the Other is no longer just like us, if ever she or he was. The Other has a different skin color, speaks a different language, and worships in a different style or manner, albeit the same God. And this point is critical. We worship the same God, however that God may be named, but allow human difference to separate and alienate us rather than draw us together. Yet, how can we seek out God while ignoring God's presence in our very midst?

Who, God, do you say that we are? If only we had the courage to ask this question of our Creator God and, more importantly, were able to be open to God's answer, our lives and our world would surely be transformed. Instead, we waste our time chasing down blind alleys, worshiping false gods of wealth and possessions, searching in strange places, listening to the voices of false prophets who promise what they cannot provide while ignoring the truth that stares us in the face. The truth is that we are one people, breathed into life by a loving God who gave us the freedom to live, prosper, multiply, and be the stewards of all of God's creation.

Who am I? What is the purpose of my being here? Is not the answer to this deeply existential question simply, God? Who am I? I am a child of God, whether black, brown, yellow, red, or white, because race does not exist in God. Nor do other divisions exist in God, not those of Muslim, Jew, Christian, Hindu, or other, because God is God for all of humanity, however God is named. No matter if one is male or female, rich or poor, young or old, we are all created in God's own image and likeness, a creation that God declared to be good without caveats. Why am I here on this earth at this time and place? To help bring about God's *kin-dom* by recognizing and, more importantly, by affirming my co-createdness with all of humanity and thus the presence of God in all with whom I come into contact. I am called, as all are called, to contribute to the rebuilding of community, a community in which all are welcome, receiving according to their needs and offering according to their abilities.

Those who are the least among us already know the answer to this most critical spiritual question for our time: "Who do you, God, say that I, humanity, am?" This is not because their lives are so simple and childlike that spirituality naturally flourishes in their midst, but because they, like Job, have been tested and survived. Their everyday lives are such a constant struggle simply to survive in the face of genocide, massacre, war, rape, poverty, and life-threatening illnesses that they are drawn ever closer to God, who is the answer to all of our longings, all of our hungers, all of our yearnings.

"Our hearts are restless until they rest in thee, O Lord." Surely, St. Augustine spoke the truth. For he too knew that lust and greed could consume one's very existence, filling one's life with supposedly all that one could wish for but somehow still leaving an echoing, gnawing emptiness within the core of one's being. This emptiness is our hunger for God, for someone or something greater than ourselves who transcends our everyday world and carries us beyond that world, enabling us to have hope.

Is it not time for us to learn from the example of those who have suffered the most and yet have a rich, nurturing life of the spirit that enables them to persevere in their daily struggle? For God is present and appears to us in the faces of those least like us, those from whom we turn away in anger, in disgust, in shame. We must learn from them. We must learn to listen to them, to work with them, to help to alleviate their suffering often caused by our greed and insensitivity. At the same time, we must try to understand who they are in themselves, rather than perceive them as objects of our charity or pity. We must also learn how, in the midst of their pain and anguish, they are still able to continue to walk and talk with God.

Difference is not dangerous; it is of God. Difference has been divinely sanctioned in the act of creation. It is our responsibility, as sharers in that creation, to turn away from divisiveness and move toward community. For, we are all our brothers' and sisters' keeper. God has placed upon all of us the responsibility of following in God's own footsteps, of loving all people as God loves us, of seeking their greater good rather than our own individual success. We can only do this by letting go of the "isms" that continue to plague humanity—negativisms based on race, ethnicity, gender, class, sexual orientation, and religious creed. We must begin to remove the blinders we have placed on ourselves that restrict our vision, blinding us to the light of God shining through the face of all God's people. We must come together as one, seeking to build a community of the faithful that rejects a narrow, dualistic perception of life.

"Who do you, God, say that we are?" We are your children, lost and wandering in a confusing and confused world, but never abandoned, never forsaken, never alone. We are your chosen ones, given knowledge of life and death, and the ability through your grace to use that knowledge to choose life in all of its diversity and to transform this world into your reign. This is our challenge for the coming century and perhaps for the new millennium. May we continue to be blessed with the wisdom and love of God in order to reclaim our full life in the Spirit and be transformed.

7

We Too Are America
Black Women's Burden of Race and Class

Zora Neale Hurston, in a memorable statement now more than fifty years old, had her fictional character, Nanny, state: "The [black] woman is the mule of the world...I been prayin' it would be different for you. Lawd, Lawd, Lawd."[1] And so black mothers and grandmothers have been praying for the sake of their daughters for over four hundred years as they have attempted to deal with the beauty but also the burden of being black and female in the United States. For to be black was seen, historically, as the antithesis of being female, of being beautiful, as African women brought to the Americas in chains quickly learned. They were everything a white woman was not and were condemned, and still are, and often severely punished for any efforts on their part to see themselves in ways that contradicted the images white society had molded for them. As historian Darlene Clark Hines states:

> The social and legal institution of slavery, which assigned ownership of slave women's bodies to their owners, of-

---

This essay was first published in *The Sky Is Crying: Race, Class, and Natural Disaster*, ed. Cheryl A. Kirk-Duggan (Nashville, TN: Abingdon Press, 2006).

ficially denied slave women the right to reject any sexual overtures and, by extension, also denied the presumption of virtue to [black women, free or slave] who often had to deal with the sexual advances of white men."[2]

In this essay, I discuss and analyze the impact of Hurricane Katrina on black people on the southern Gulf Coast of the United States, especially African American women. Employing a womanist historical-critical methodology, rooted in the particular historical experience of African American women, I explore how black women, as depicted on the cover of every major U.S. and foreign newsmagazine, were the true face of this tragedy. Such recognition reveals the ongoing disgrace of U.S. unwillingness to confront and systematically deal with the overlapping issues of race, class, and gender in the United States. Throughout the weeks after the devastation, many questioned the impact of race, class, and gender as factors in the poor preplanning, the failure to ensure that all could safely evacuate, the scapegoating of black Americans as thugs and predators, and the slow response of the federal government.

Sociocultural, Historical Context: Creating Black Savagery

Today, some four centuries after the beginnings of the enslavement of persons of African descent in this country, black women, their children, and their men are still too often seen as the antithesis of humanity. Their blackness, their strength, their coping skills, their ability to survive all that was inflicted upon them led Euro-Americans to see blacks as quintessentially "Other." During slavery, that otherness was the basis for their enslavement, savage but tamable children who needed guidance and care if they were to survive in the "New World" to which they had been forcibly and involuntarily brought. Slavery's aftermath, and the freeing of blacks in the South, led to a re-drawing of their "otherness," one which cast a dark and evil gaze upon black men and women, rendering them as savages, incapable of being civilized, a danger to those who had sought to keep them under control. In either case, dominant culture saw them as less than human, barely civilized savages, incapable of self-control. Thus, it is not surprising that once blacks were herded like beasts into a dark, dank arena, the Superdome, and left without resources of any kind, the rumors (most of which have since been disproved) of a people running wild, raping, killing, fighting one another for the little food and water that existed, began to spread, accompanied by other stories, avidly fed on by the media and too easily believed by many, of a city overrun by gangsters who were indiscriminately looting, killing, and attacking everyone in sight.[3] Logistically, this was impossible, of course, but it led to the halting of search and rescue missions so that the city could be "recaptured" from the comparatively small number of thugs while starving family members were arrested for taking diapers, infant formula, water, milk, and other items from stores that were themselves destroyed by the storm and its aftermath. This is how people are demonized, are rendered inhuman, and are therefore left open to scapegoating and further neglect.

Images of the black savage, usually male but also female, are still a part of the cultural history of the United States as generation after generation is exposed to the dangerous black man and the lazy welfare queen. Stereotyped and stigmatized, black men and women and their children, who in cartoons that entertained millions were depicted as idiotic and animalistic,[4] are still seen in the United States as less than others simply because of the color of their skin. If anyone doubts this statement or sees it as overly broad, they need simply to read the media and governmental depictions that proliferated in the aftermath of Hurricane Katrina.

Katrina was not an act of God but a powerful manifestation of nature's wrath. Its horrific impact was a result of humanity's indifference and greed. Those who suffered were of every race and ethnicity, but it cannot and should not be denied that those who felt the brunt of the hurricane and especially its aftermath were the poor who, in New Orleans and throughout the Gulf region, were predominately black and female. Hispanics and Native Americans were also severely affected, but because of this nation's historical, and often hysterical, fascination with all things black,[5] they were the ones seen, heard, and ignored as well as demonized on national television.

Some Facts: Mapping the Poverty; Naming the Oppression and the Disregard

New Orleans was almost 65 percent black before Katrina hit. The unemployment rate in New Orleans was almost double that of the nation, and for blacks it was even higher; 35 percent were un-employed. More than 20 percent of residents of New Orleans lived under the U.S. poverty line, most of them women with children. More than 100,000 or 20 percent of the population had no access to any form of motorized transportation because they did not own cars, and learned too late that Greyhound and Amtrak were no longer operating in New Orleans.[6] The only way out was by car—if you were able to find enough gas—or by foot. Yet even that mode was not open to the many who were physically or mentally disabled, sick in hospitals or at home, elderly, or too young. Those who tried found quickly as the waters rose that their neighbors in outlying suburbs accessible by the Crescent City Bridge were not open to their efforts to flee; instead, rows of police with weapons in hand greeted them with a cruelty that was breathtaking. They wanted nothing to do with those fleeing for their lives, fearing they would overrun their towns.

> If anyone doubted that there were two Americas, this dis-aster has made those divisions clear. The victims have been largely poor and Black. The devastation from Hurricane Katrina only underscores the disastrous consequences of

the Administration's failure to take even the most basic
steps to alleviate poverty in the U.S. The Administration
cannot ignore this reality.[7]

As the waters rose and people frantically took shelter in the
Superdome and the Convention Center in New Orleans or
scrambled up into their hot and sealed attics, the nation
watched as its president went to a birthday party, played a gift
guitar, and only after four days of flooding, with reluctance
ended his five-week vacation two days early and deigned to do
a fly-over of the now drowned city.

What transpired in New Orleans should not have come as
a surprise to anyone. It had long been predicted but at the same
time ignored. Efforts by parishes [counties] and the Corps of
Engineers to rebuild, shore up, or in other ways strengthen and
stabilize the levee system protecting the city had been under-
funded for years, coincidentally the years of the Bush Administration and the wars in Iraq and Afghanistan. Local politicians
even admitted as did the *New Orleans Times-Picayune* over several years, from 2001 to 2005, that funds intended for the city's
protection had been cut and re-directed to these wars as well as
to supporting the tax cuts and other gifts to the wealthy that
the heavily Republican Congress supported.[8] Yet this story of
neglect is even older. Senator Barack Obama was quoted as saying: "I hope we realize that the people of New Orleans were
not just abandoned during the hurricane. They were abandoned long ago—to murder and mayhem on the streets, to
substandard schools, to dilapidated housing, to inadequate
health care, to a pervasive sense of hopelessness."[9]

The poor and black in New Orleans experienced neglect in
all of its forms as the city flourished as a sought-after site for con-
ventions and conferences. They were the ones who enabled
these events to run smoothly, especially the women who made
sure the beds and rooms of hotel guests were clean and properly
prepared, who cooked behind the scenes while the chefs took

the credit, who worked long hours as servers in restaurants and fast-food establishments, yet who often had not enough to feed their children and clothe them properly but somehow they did. One of the comments made by a black woman who once knew what it was like to be poor and neglected struck me as I watched the unfolding horror of that long week. Oprah Winfrey, who toured the Houston Astrodome where thousands had been relocated, wondered at and admired the hair of little black girls whose mothers, in order to keep themselves sane as best they could, made sure their sons and daughters were clean, their hair neatly braided and pinned up with bows, braid, ribbons, even string, whatever they could put their hands on to help their children and the children, quite often, of those they collected along the way, maintain their dignity and self-respect. Yet, Barbara Bush, mother of the president, likened their experience of near death by drowning, starvation, and dehydration and their current life in the Astrodome without privacy or proper facilities for eating and sleeping as a step up for the underprivileged.[10]

Loretta Ross made a powerful statement on the Z-Net (*Z Magazine*) online, on October 10, 2005.

> Poverty in America is not only racialized but it is also gendered. The aftermath of Katrina must be examined through a gender lens that identifies the myriad of violations experienced by women. A disaster like Katrina is a violation against the entire community, but when threats to women's lives are not recognized, and steps are not taken to ensure that they are, women become doubly victimized—by the disaster and by the response to it.
>
> The hurricane and the subsequent flooding exposed the specific vulnerability of woman, children, the elderly, and the disabled by revealing the harsh intersections of race, class, gender, ability, and life expectancy. Many people could not escape not only because of poverty, but because they were not physically able to

punch through rooftops, perch on top of buildings, or climb trees to survive.[11]

Initially, the media and government at every level sought to place blame on those who died for making incorrect or poor choices. The truth is that many who died in their attics and living rooms, who found themselves abandoned in the Superdome without food, water, and medicines, or dumped and left stranded on Interstate 10 in blazing heat for more than four days had no choices. They found themselves at the mercy of others who should have taken the responsibility to ensure their safety but who, like Pontius Pilate (Matt 27:15–26), washed their hands and thereby washed away the lives of thousands, asserting that they had to use their own initiative to escape the rising waters. Some even sought to blame single black mothers for their plight, admonishing them that if they had married the father of their children, they would have had higher economic status and would therefore not have suffered as they did. This notion, of course, ignores the fact that white and Hispanic women are also increasingly having children without marrying; for some it is a matter of choice, for others a matter of immigration, but for none is it a willful decision to choose poverty for themselves and their children rather than marry. In actuality, however, there has been a significant decline in teenage pregnancies since the early 1960s, especially among African American girls, signifying greater rather than less responsibility on their parts.[12]

Again this is not new, but the same sad and horrific story played out now in the twenty-first century. Alisa Bierria, writing in the September 11, 2005, newsletter of *Incite! Women of Color Against Violence,* spoke painfully of "memories of hurricanes and floods past in New Orleans [that] help put Katrina in a historical perspective."[13] Her mother lived through Hurricane Camille, which hit New Orleans in 1969. As the waters rose in their home, her father and other men hurriedly smashed wooden barrels to build emergency makeshift rafts to save families from drowning. In 1927, the Great Mississippi Flood poured down into New Orleans, provoking white people to round up black people and force them into work camps run by armed guards. Black people were prevented from leaving, though the flooding had already begun. Some black people were held at gunpoint and used as human sand bags to keep the levees from breaking. New Orleans has a history of black bravery and ingenuity, as well as of violent racism in the face of environmental disaster.[14]

Biarria concludes:

> And as I am searching for ways to deal with this current disaster, I am also feeling a familiar rage that I felt after September 11, 2001. A terrible knowledge in my gut that this devastation could have been avoided if it had not been for actions of my government.
>
> But I am seeking out hope and I am turning my rage into organizing because I refuse to give up on my people.[15]

The Women: Like Hagar,
Working for a Quality of Life in Community

Bierria's words are ones that echo down through the generations of black women who, forced to live lives seemingly bereft of all hope, still managed to reach down within themselves and bring forth not just hope but the courage to "keep on keepin' on" despite all that they had to deal with. Shorn of their right to the respect and dignity promised by God to all of God's creation (Gen 1), black women, often at risk of their own lives, somehow made a path that those coming after them could walk. They fought against the diminution and degradation of not just slavery but also Jim Crow segregation and all other efforts by their fellow Christians and others in the United States to deny them their rightful place in the human race and as U.S.

citizens. Many were lynched; even more were raped and forced to bear children for the profit of their owners. But they resisted as best they could and, most important, they lived to pass on the knowledge and wisdom needed for black people to survive. Theirs was not and is not today an easy path to walk. Black women have truly, as Hurston noted, borne the burdens that others refused to bear, but they did so in order to ensure the survival of black humanity in the United States.

Delores Williams asserts in her discussion of Hagar, the concubine of Abram and the slave of Sarai, that black women had to work out their liberation in ways that were different from that of their men. Liberation was the final goal, but in order to achieve it, black women had to first deal with issues of survival and quality of life.[16] What is the point of freedom if it is only for oneself and is at the cost of others? What kind of life is it if it is lived in barracks-like stadiums, in cities and states far from one's home, and without the barest of life's necessities to enable one to at least have some hope of a better day?

> The term quality of life ... refers to persons, families, and/or communities attempting to arrive at well-being through the use of, search for and/or creation of supportive spiritual, economic, political, legal or educational resources ... In the context of much black American religious faith, survival struggle and quality-of-life struggle are inseparable and are associated with God's presence in the community.[17]

This mindset obviously flies in the face of today's overemphasis on individualism and "I gotta get mine" ideologies that are systematically destroying all forms of community life in the United States. Black women have historically sacrificed themselves for their men and their children. Although today that is no longer necessary, nor was it ever fully legitimate or healthy, as black men and women have been able to climb out of the ghetto through education and other means, the emphasis on communal rather than individual success is still a critical aspect of black women's lives.

Alice Walker recognized this when she coined the word "womanist" in the early 1980s, which provided a framework that gave birth to a spiritual and theological movement that continues to develop to this day.[18] Cheryl Townsend Gilkes describes Walker's efforts:

> Alice Walker introduced the word *Womanist* in 1982 when she sought an alternative word for organizing our thinking about black women's self-definitions, relationships, activities, and history and their meaning for the black experience. To my mind, her dictionary style definition offered a grounded theory of black women's culture that was constructed out of the dialogues within the fundamental female-female relationship of any culture, mothers and daughters, and the distinctive values ("loves") that she observed in the world of black women. Walker's definition asserts the existence of a black women's culture that values not only women and women's relationships but the men and the "entire community male and female." Walker identifies a fundamental commitment to the "survival and wholeness" of this community as a hallmark of this Womanist idea.[19]

And the Beat Goes On: Black Women, Too, Sing America

There are many questions that still need answering after Hurricane Katrina. In the largest involuntary dispersal of humanity quite possibly in U.S. history, we must ask what will happen to those who were snatched from their daily lives, lost all that they had, including proof of their identity, and were unceremoniously evacuated and dispersed throughout the country. The scenes brought back memories of slave auctions where men, women, and children were separated from each other and thrown into the back of wagons or led away on foot while the screams and despairing cries of their loved ones echoed in their ears. Just as, in the aftermath of the Civil War, thousands of African Americans took to dusty roads in the South seeking to find a beloved mother, a lost child, a missing husband or wife, so today many are still struggling to reconnect, attempting to find out who lived or died, where their children are, and what is to become of them. Some fear that it is the hope of many that they will settle where they were dispersed, becoming a problem for other states. But how do you rebuild a life without friends, lovers, and family in areas where no one looks, acts, or speaks like you or fully understands your plight? African Americans were forced to do this over and over again during and after slavery; must they walk this road again? The fear is that their homes, flooded and now polluted with mold and death, will be destroyed and, unable to make a claim without papers, they will lose even the property they owned as re-gentrification takes place, replacing poor blacks with higher income whites. Can this really be happening in the twenty-first century?

Yet somehow, I believe, those who have been dispersed will return, perhaps not in the same numbers but in sufficient numbers to demand that they be included in the decisions being made about the rebuilding of New Orleans; for New Orleans without African Americans will not be the same city. They built this city with their blood, sweat, and tears during slavery; they created tapestries in wrought iron; they flavored it with their gumbos and red beans and rice; they spiced it with jazz and the second line. African Americans are the roux that makes the city of New Orleans. Without them, it will be flat and tasteless and the tourists will not return.

But, most important, the women must come back. As Cheryl Townsend Gilkes notes, "if it wasn't for the women,"[20] there would be no black community, in New Orleans or anywhere else in the United States.

I have concluded that black women are fundamentally correct in their self-assessment: "If it wasn't for the women," the black community would not have the churches and other organizations that have fostered the psychic and material survival of individuals and that have mobilized the constituencies that have produced change and progress. At every level of social interaction and cultural production women are present, and at the same time they are conscious of the way the dominant white society disrespects and rejects their presence. Furthermore, white society historically has communicated that disrespect and rejection through a wide variety of stereotypes that have invited shame and exhortations that black women change their behavior.[21]

Loretta Ross asserts therefore:

To counter this, women must seize our power and make our concerns known in the media, to government agencies, and to the humanitarian organizations...Women must ask critical questions during this crisis. Who are the groups benefiting from this crisis and who are the groups hurting or excluded...? We need to demand economic re-development strategies that center our needs, not those of casino owners, in the picture...We have to claim our human right to sustainable development and insist on the enforcement of economic and social strategies. We have the right to quality schools for our children, jobs that pay living wages, communities free of environmental toxins, and opportunities to develop our full human potential. We have the right to reclaim our land, rebuild our homes, and restore our communities.[22]

Sadly, many of the Gulf Coast historical records of the efforts of black women to sustain life and promote community have now been lost for the most part as a result of Katrina. The archives of the second oldest religious order of black Catholic women, the Holy Family Sisters (1851) were flooded along with their motherhouse, their nursing home, and their schools. Their very existence was almost washed away, as were the records of the only black Catholic university in this country, Xavier University, most of whose buildings suffered serious damage. Dillard, Southern, and so many other black universities that thrived in New Orleans have been seriously damaged, but I have no doubt they will all over time recover. We are a resilient people, steeped in faith in a God who is a "wonder-working" God who will "make a way out of no way." We recognize and affirm that we are and have been a critical part of this country since its earliest beginnings and can, therefore, affirm with Langston Hughes that we not only can "sing America,"[23] but that we also are America in its fullest sense.

NOTES

1. *Their Eyes Were Watching God* (New York: Harper & Row Perennial Library Edition, 1990), 14.

2. Darlene Clark Hine, ed., *Black Women in America: An Historical Encyclopedia* (Bloomington: Indiana University Press, 1994), 457.

3. See September 12, 2005, issues of *Newsweek*, *Time*, and *U.S. News and World Report*.

4. See, for example, the film *Ethnic Notions*, directed by Marlon Riggs and narrated by Esther Rolle (California Newsreel 1986).

5. See Robert E. Hood, *Begrimed and Black: Christian Traditions on Blacks and Blackness* (Minneapolis: Fortress Press, 1994).

6. *Newsweek*, "A Special Report: After Katrina," *Newsweek* 146, no. 11 (September 12, 2005): 30.

7. A statement issued by the office of Congresswoman Barbara Lee, September 2, 2005, quoted on the same day in *Time Out*, an online news and politics journal, www.timeout.com.

8. *Newsweek*, "A Special Report: After Katrina," 46.

9. John Alter, "The Other America," *Newsweek* 146, no. 12 (September 19, 2005): 43.

10. Ibid., 44.

11. "A Feminist Perspective on Katrina," www.zmag.org (October 10, 2005).

12. Ruth Rosen, "Get Hitched, Young Woman" by TomPaine.com (Common Dreams Newscenter, Sept. 26, 2005), www.common-dreams.org/view05/0926-32.htm.

13. Alissa Bierria in the newsletter of *Incite! Women of Color Against Violence*, www.incite-national.org/issues/katrina.html.

14. Ibid. This disaster, like Katrina, displaced thousands of African Americans, many of whom stayed in the North, which resulted in a massive redistribution of blacks and later led to the shifting of many blacks from the Republican to the Democratic political party because of the former party's failure to live up to its promises. For more, see John Barry, *Rising Tide: The Great Mississippi Flood of 1927 and How It Changed America* (New York: Simon and Schuster, 1998).

15. Ibid.

16. Delores Williams, *Sisters in the Wilderness* (Maryknoll, NY: Orbis Books, 1993).

17. Ibid., 246.

18. Alice Walker, *In Search of Our Mother's Gardens: Womanist Prose* (New York: Harcourt Brace Jovanovich, 1983).

19. Cheryl Townsend Gilkes, *If It Wasn't for the Women* (Maryknoll, NY: Orbis Books, 2001), 10.

20. Ibid.

21. Ibid., 7.

22. Ross, "A Feminist Perspective on Katrina."

23. See Langston Hughes, "I, Too," in *The Collected Poems of Langston Hughes*, ed. Arnold Rampersad (New York: Alfred A. Knopf, 1994), 46. In the title of my essay, I have used America in keeping with its usage in Hughes's poem, while recognizing that America denotes both North and South America.

8

Woman Offered #5

From time immemorial, women, of all races and ethnicities, of all classes, have been nailed to the cross of Jesus Christ. Willingly, even eagerly, some have climbed up and hung, believing that in doing so their sacrifice of love, their martyrdom, will protect them, their families, and especially their children. Others, unwilling and unasked, have been forced onto their crosses by those they love and by the societies in which they live, again for their own protection and the good of society. In reality, they are crucified solely because they are women and that, the world teaches, is the role of women—to sacrifice themselves, their hopes, dreams, and aspirations for everyone.

Come down from the cross! If Jesus were to return today, would these not be some of the first words he would say to our world? "Come down; stop sacrificing yourselves for your alleged sins and those of others. It is no sin to be a woman; it is a grace, given by God. I died so that no one, no one, would ever have to suffer the cruel pain of crucifixion, of dying, hanging from a tree, stabbed, starved, laughed at, and derided. Come down off that cross, now! Do not wait for others to take you down; you have the right and the ability to stop your suffering yourself! Come Down!"

This reflection was first published in *Holiness and the Feminine Spirit: The Art of Janet McKenzie*, ed, Susan Perry (Maryknoll, NY: Orbis Books, 2009): 81–84.

Too many women have been "surrogate sufferers," forced to live lives of sacrifice and self-effacement for the supposed good of others, especially their men, rather than being able to freely choose paths of their own making, lives of their own choosing, futures of their own desiring. They have been placed on crosses, however they may be named, that imprison rather than liberate, that impede rather than promote, that weaken rather than empower, and that cripple rather than strengthen. Motherhood and martyrdom, the virgin or the whore, these have been the extremely limited roles available to women. Any woman who chooses another way, seeking to serve God in her own right, whether by remaining single but not in religious life, by seeking further education beyond domestic skills or approved women's fields that initially, like nursing and teaching, were also forbidden to them, is condemned as "unnatural," prideful, and even persecuted as a witch.

The cross has become historically not a symbol of a once-and-for-all freely given sacrifice of life and love but a punishment for women, the poor, persons of color, all and any who dare to be different because they are born different, as we all are born. Those historically marginalized and made voiceless in our world, the majority of whom are women, must now step down from the cross. This is not why Jesus died and rose again. He died and rose again to give life, not take it away. He died to open up our lives to their limitless possibilities and not to restrict them by negativity, self-doubt, or fear.

Women have been condemned for their intelligence, for their sexuality, for their emotions, all gifts given to them in their creation by a God of love and compassion. God created women not as scapegoats or footstools, not as baby-making machines or mindless beings, robots without wills of their own. No. God created woman to work in solidarity with God's other creation, man; to stand alongside and not in back or in front of him, to care for all of God's creation. Both creation stories confirm this. The first chapter of Genesis states that God created male and female at the same time as the pinnacle of God's creation (Gen 1:26), to nurture and sustain it, not to dominate or destroy it. But many know nothing of this story because the emphasis of Christian churches has always been on the story of Adam and Eve.

Even there we do not find a mandate for woman to be submissive to the will of man. Both are meant to submit to the will of God and both fail to do so, in their own way. Eve is Adam's help-mate, a term too often misinterpreted as servant or slave, rather than one who works in harmony with him as an equal. They do not have ownership of each other or of God's creation; they are stewards, not masters. They have the ability, by the grace of God, to think for themselves and, in doing so, as many of us finite humans continue to do to this day, they strayed from God's path. They were punished by banishment but they were not cursed. More important, their banishment freed them to create life themselves in their own image and likeness and that of God's, again by the compassionate grace of God. They were freed to cultivate the land, to attain knowledge of themselves and the world around them. In other words, they were freed to be human. Eve was not the source of evil or the gateway to hell. She was and continues to be the source of life as we have come to know it in its purest and fullest sense.

Women are the bearers of life and culture. They tell the stories, sing the songs, reweave the tapestries of our lives, and pass on knowledge of life and the world around them to all of humanity. Their gifts should be celebrated rather than condemned, rewarded rather than punished, proclaimed rather than ignored. Jesus himself proclaimed in Mark 14:9 of the unknown woman who anointed him, "I assure you that wherever the gospel is preached all over the world, what she has done will be told in memory of her."

The gospel has been preached for two millennia, but somehow this passage has been ignored, in much the same way that the role of women in Jesus' ministry and their proclaiming of the gospel message have been ignored. Instead, we hear only of women who are sinners or martyrs, virgins or whores. Where are the real women living real lives of love, friendship, study, writing, preaching, prophesying, dancing, praying, and singing? We know little of them.

Women, of every race and nation, have carried the weight of the world on their shoulders from time immemorial. They have suffered long enough for the sins and failings of everyone. It is time, long past time, for them to come down from the cross and walk freely into new life, a life of possibility, not pain, of progress, not false failures. This does not mean that they can walk away from responsibility toward themselves and others but that they have the freedom to choose for themselves the paths they should take, the lives they should lead, the tapestries they will weave. All adults, male and female, should be free to choose. They are free to envision different possibilities for themselves and, therefore, for those they love.

Woman! Come down from that cross! It is not yours to bear. Jesus was nailed to the cross, died, and rose again, making the cross a symbol of resurrection, not of pain or death. Lift up your head, look the world straight in the eye, and come down from the cross to take up your life as God's beloved, weaving a new world, free of pain and suffering, hatred, prejudice and discrimination, oppression and marginalization, into a new, complex, and fruitful life.

Come down!

9

Faith of Our Mothers

Catholic Womanist God-Talk

She is clothed with strength and dignity,
And she laughs at the days to come.
She opens her mouth in wisdom,
And on her tongue is kindly counsel.

—Proverbs 31:25–26

It can be said, arguably, that I am using these verses somewhat out of context, for they are taken from a section of Proverbs that describes the "ideal wife"! But my purpose is not to consider the qualities of the "ideal wife" but to consider how for centuries in the United States especially, women of color, and especially African American women, whether Protestant or Catholic, were seen as "ideal" only as models for slavery, sexual abuse, racial discrimination, and any and all other forms of degradation and dehumanization. Yet, somehow they remained women "clothed with strength and dignity" who, through their shared wisdom and that of their ancestors, were instrumental in not only pre-

---

First published in M. Shawn Copeland, ed., *Uncommon Faithfulness: The Black Catholic Experience* (Maryknoll, NY: Orbis Books, 2009), 129–46.

serving themselves but in building up and preserving the black community as a whole, women, men, and children.

The daughters of Africa, who now make their home in the United States, have had almost five hundred years in which to be perfected as women of God. They came, nameless and unknown, identified only as "Negro woman, age about 6 or 12 or 22." They may have come with family and/or friends caught up in the sudden invasion of their village life and the daily round of farming or grazing, cooking and weaving, or they came alone, sharing little but fear of the unknown with those captured and traded with them.

New relationships were forged as they were thrown, often unclothed, always defenseless, into the holds of countless ships with names like "Jesus" or "Blessed Redeemer" but which they saw and experienced as floating hells, places of licentiousness and terror, as they were raped, fed slops, and often, at the first sign of the "bloody flux," thrown overboard alive, food for the always accompanying sharks.

When they landed, offloaded from the "big canoe" that had taken them over the "river without banks," they found their situations had not improved but, if possible, had even worsened. They were separated from family and friends, from those who understood their language or shared their culture, and sold to men with lust in their eyes, to serve as breeders, field hands, wet nurses, and maids of all work. Cuffed and shackled, they were taken to distant farms and plantations and quickly realized that this was to be their fate in life: to work from "can't see to can't see"; to be treated as farm animals, mere beasts of labor; to be bred with strangers; to give birth only to see their offspring sold away from them over and over again. In other words, to live and die as property. Not for them was the protected pedestal of "true womanhood." They were not seen as "ideal" women or wives, even for their fellow slaves. This myth, used to protect but also confine white women, "stressed piety, purity, submissiveness, and domesticity for women as well as innocence and modesty."[1] African American women, however, were not included in this understanding, as they were required to work in the same fields as their men. At the same time, purity and innocence were unattainable, because of the uses to which they were put by greedy men and unscrupulous women.

> The social and legal institution of slavery, which assigned ownership of slave women's bodies to their owners, officially denied slave women the right to reject any sexual overtures and, by extension, also denied the presumption of virtue to [black women—free or slave] who often had to deal with the sexual advances of white men.[2]

Yet they did not despair nor did they turn away from all hope. They had not come empty handed to this new world but brought with them a deep and abiding faith in a God of creation, a God of justice and honor, however God was named in their particular communities. They were survivors, not in the silly sense of today's so-called reality shows, but in the deepest sense of those who survived experiences conducive only to death. Hagar, the slave woman and concubine of Abraham, exemplifies black women's experience of survival. For Hagar experiences what Delores Williams calls the "wilderness experience," an experience that all African Americans have shared in slavery and afterwards. Hagar's experience revealed the wilderness not as something to be overcome or conquered but as a place of refuge. In her first wilderness experience, Hagar

> meets *her* God for the first time. Her experience with this God could be regarded as positive by African

Americans because God promises survival, freedom, and nationhood for Hagar's progeny. The African American community has, all of its life, struggled for survival, freedom, and nationhood.[3]

But Hagar's experience, like that of most slave women, does not end here. She is forced to return to the wilderness as a free woman with her child but without resources of any kind, just as the slaves experienced a "freedom" in name only at Reconstruction's end as they had nothing but themselves.

Like African American people, Hagar and her child are alone without resources for survival. Hagar must try to make a living in the wide, wide world for herself and her child. This was also the task of many African American women and the entire community of black freed people when emancipation came.[4]

Williams continues:

The post-bellum notion of wilderness (with Hagar and child as its content) emphasized black women's and the black community's negative economic experience of poverty and social displacement . . . This post-bellum African American symbolic sense of wilderness, with Hagar at its center, makes the female figure symbolic of the entire black community's history of brutalization during slavery; of fierce survival struggle and servitude after liberation; of children being cheated out of their inheritance by oppressors; of threat to the life and well-being of the family; of the continuing search for a positive, productive quality of life for women and men under God's care.[5]

It is not known how many of the millions of Africans who endured the middle passage to the Americas were Catholic Christians (converted and baptized by the Portuguese from the fifteenth century on), Muslims, or followers of the traditional African religions. What is known is that they brought with them a shared worldview which, when later syncretized with the Christian faith of their captors, enabled them to persevere, sustained by their belief in a "wonder working" God who would, in God's own time, free them from the unmerited captivity in which they passed their weary existence.

Brought from the western lands of Africa, people of many tribes, cultures, and languages yet shared a worldview that enabled them to survive four hundred plus years of slavery, segregation, discrimination, and second-class citizenship. This worldview was sacred, resisting the dualistic separation of the sacred and secular domains that their captors/enslavers sought to instill in them. African women and men "knew" God intimately as active, either as God-self or through intermediaries, in their everyday lives, and that knowledge nurtured and sustained them. Religion was seen as all pervasive, surrounding them on all sides. The holy was a constant presence in their lives and all of life was sacred, from womb to tomb, before and beyond, weaving a web of connections that encompassed both the living and the dead. This religious understanding helped them to create community, for individualism was not a part of their self-understanding. Rather, the "I" of the individual was seen to exist and persist only in the "we" of family and friends—blood and fictive kin who played substantial roles in their lives and the lives of their descendants. They took this understanding and wove it into their reception of the God of Jesus Christ who, they believed, had suffered like them and shared in their pain. This God, who had himself been whipped and lynched, had freed others wrongly enslaved and, despite the insistence of their owners that God had willed their captive status, they knew that God would in time free them as well.

Black women are a critical part of this understanding, for they are the "bearers of culture," those who passed on the stories, the songs, the prayers, and the memories of the people. They were able to form a connection that, rather than being broken, was strengthened and expanded in the Americas to encompass all who were enslaved.

> [Women] were the heads of their communities, the keepers of the tradition. The lives of these women were defined by their culture, the needs of the community and the people they served. Their lives are available to us today because they accepted responsibility when the opportunity was offered—when they were chosen. There is the element of transformation in all of their work. Building communities within societies that enslaved Africans, they and their people had to exist in, at least, dual realities. These women, however, became central to evolving the structures for resolving areas of conflict and maintaining, sometimes creating, an identity that was independent of a society organized to exploit natural resources, people, and land.[6]

These structures remain to this day as symbols of the strength, courage, and steadfast faith of these nameless and unknown African women who laid the foundation for the millions who followed them.

The majority of black Catholics came speaking Spanish or French as well as their native languages except for those, fewer in number and later in their arrival, who came with the English Catholic settlers to the colony of Maryland. Most came long before others from Africa, beginning as early as the sixteenth century, and were both free and slave.

> The first Africans to arrive in what is now the conti-
> nental United States were Spanish-speaking and
> Roman Catholic. The Spanish government introduced
> in 1565 the colony of St. Augustine in northern
> Florida . . . The baptismal registers, which began with
> the colony and are the oldest ecclesiastical documents
> in American history, witness to the presence of Blacks
> among the first inhabitants of St. Augustine. In these
> registers, Blacks and mulattos are clearly designated as
> such, along with the indication of whether the individ-
> ual was slave or free.[7]

Today we are just beginning to uncover and explore the
histories, the stories, of the women of this and other Catholic
colonies. They are our mothers, our heroes; women who somehow, despite all of the forces arrayed against them, were able to
not simply preserve a culture but to pass it on to those coming
after them. We know very little about black Catholic women,
free or slave, except for the names found in those old baptismal
and marriage records. But, as Fr. Davis remarks, these clearly
noted who was black or mulatto, quadroon or some other mix
of Africa with the Native peoples of this "new world" to which
they had been brought as well as the blood of their captors and
oppressors, the Europeans, whether French, Spanish, or Eng-
lish-speaking. We know they were co-founders of cities but we
also know them as women who worked long hours and seemingly impossible jobs in order to keep their families intact, their
children baptized and catechized, and their faith strong in the
face of opposition from so many within their own church as
well as society.

Their full story is not yet written partly because the stories
of all women, regardless of race or ethnicity, have historically
been ignored for centuries. In the case of black Catholic
women, however, it is also because there were so few able to

recover or interested in recovering these histories. It is only in the aftermath of the Second Vatican Council that we begin to see, as a result of increasing numbers of black Catholic women entering into theological programs of study, efforts to uncover, recover, and proclaim these and other critical stories. It is vital that we do so for they are the foundation for the black Catholic community today, women who worked side by side with black Catholic men, but who also had the courage and foresight to come together as women in the church today to struggle for change.

They were lay and religious, slave and free, women like Henriette De Lille and Elizabeth Lange, founders of religious orders who chose to live lives of obedience to God rather than as concubines or servants, whose stories finally have been written and published. They also include women like Coincoin, a former slave and successful plantation owner who, after receiving her freedom and that of one of her ten children, spent the rest of her life purchasing the freedom of the remainder as well as all of her grandchildren. We also call forth the names of Ellen Terry, who established Catholic settlement houses in the East and Midwest; and Dr. Lena Edwards, the first board-certified African American female obstetrician and gynecologist. You could say that they all had a dream, a dream of a time when Catholics of African descent would not only be welcomed in their church as full and equal participants in God's mission but would also be leaders, honored for their contributions to the life of the church at every level. Through their perseverance in faith, these women, the "bearers of culture" as all women are, gave birth to a people and a world that persists to this day. As Fr. Cyprian affirms, speaking of black Catholic religious women:

> In a time when black people were accorded little or no respect or esteem, in a time when black women were

degraded by slaveholders or abused by white employ-
ers, in a society where women were considered to be
weak in morality, black sisters were a counter-sign and
a proof that the black Catholic community was rooted
in faith and devotion; for vocations arise from a faith-
filled people. Lest it be forgotten, the two black sisterhoods were not European transplants; they were very
much American in origin.[8]

These women were mothers in the fullest sense of the
word, one not limited by biological or blood-ties. They were
mothers to an entire people seeking through the work that
they did to enable them to survive and thrive. As Fr. Davis
states: "the African American religious sisterhoods helped lay
the faith foundation of the black Catholic community... As pi-
oneers, they often worked without encouragement or support
and too often in the face of indifference and antipathy. Without them, the black Catholic community would not be what it
is today."[9]

But the sisters were not entirely alone in their struggle.
They were joined and supported by black Catholic mothers
who, within their families, the domestic church, not only
planted the seeds of faith but nurtured them until they
bloomed into black Catholic men and women determined to
carve out a niche for themselves and their people, not only in
the Catholic Church but in the United States as well. It is the
lives of faith of these women that serve as the source from
which Catholic Womanist Theology springs forth.

Womanist theologians use the "stuff" of women's lives
to spin a narrative of their persistent effort to rise above
and beyond those persons and situations which attempt
to hold them down. Their sources are social, political,
anthropological, and, especially, literary.[10]

Womanist theology, a theology historically of, by, and for black Christian women acting to build (and rebuild) community, emerged at a critical time in the history of Christianity and the world, a time of revolutionary change in which "the least among us" began to take charge of their own lives and, as a result, of how their stories were told and their faith life presented. It is a theology that seeks to bring women of African descent in the United States to voice by enabling them to "speak the truth" of their historical and contemporary experiences as black and Catholic women to the people, a truth both bitter and sweet; one that relates how they were able to "make it through."

The term "womanist" comes, of course, from the poet and author Alice Walker who sought a descriptive term for "audacious, courageous, bold and daring" black women that did not restrict them with definitions already developed and concretized by others who had not shared their experiences nor require them to place a "color" before their names to distinguish them from normative society. To be womanist is to be black; to be black is to be womanist, at least as the term has become not simply defined but developed and deepened by black female Christian theologians such as Delores Williams, Jacqueline Grant, and Kelly Brown Douglas among others. A critical response to the absent voice of women of color in both feminist (normatively white) and black (normatively male) liberation theologies, womanist theology seeks to bring the presence and activity of black women to the forefront, rather than the background, of the church's awareness and dialogue.

Both Protestant and Catholic theologians have helped to deepen our understanding of this term, in keeping with the ongoing endeavor in which all theologians are ostensibly engaged, the effort of "faith seeking understanding" in such a way that the faith can be explicated for others. It is an exercise in "doing" theology, praxis rather than merely "thinking" without putting the results of that reflection into action. It is an exercise that engages heart, mind, and spirit in the effort to correlate the historical experience of all black folk—man, woman, or child—with the gospel. Thus, womanist theology is also a theology of liberation. It both liberates those "doing" that theology, turning them from the objects they have been made into by others into subjects of their own histories. As well, womanist theology liberates theology itself from the rigid, top-down stranglehold of abstraction and objectivity that, for centuries, has been its captivity, enabling theology to speak on behalf of those unjustly wronged and dehumanized as Jesus himself did.

Womanist theology starts with black women, women of African descent, in their own particular situations. It engages their historical experience, a very brief example of which I gave above, and seeks to reorient reality through the eyes of a black woman. Womanist theologians, Protestant and Catholic, seek to speak a new language, a God-talk that is borne out of a centuries' long struggle to be free women, seen and affirmed as being created in the image and likeness of God. Womanist God-talk, thus, springs from centuries of denigration and dehumanization, from the denial of our female persons and the right to control our own bodies, minds, and spirits. It is a struggle that continues into the present day, a struggle to articulate what it means to be a black woman, and more particularly for me, a black Catholic woman, in the world and in the church today. It is also a theology that seeks to confront not just race, or class, or gender, or sexuality or any other forms of oppression that continue to flourish into the twenty-first century but all of these, reflecting the dualistic separation of one form of oppression from another that has kept people who share in oppression apart from one another instead of in solidarity against the status quo. This is because black women have experienced and continue to experience all of these oppressions in their own bodies and lives, in their families and communities. Oppression cannot be dealt with singly; it must be attacked like the virus it is, one that simply mutates and changes form as it moves from one place and one people to another. It can only be eradicated when it is attacked from every angle, addressing all of its venomous reality.

As women of African descent, we look first to Africa as the cradle of our history, culture, and traditions, seeking to tap into that river of spirituality that flowed through our ancestors and enabled them to survive the Middle Passage, Jim Crow, segregated pews and segregated sacraments, and still speak a word of life and hope to those coming after them.

There is a "generational continuity" (the passing on of cultural values and personal history), which is traditionally the domain of women which can be seen to continue today as black women writers, for example, focus "on Africa not only as historical ancestor, political ally, and basis for ideological stance but as part of a continuum in which Black women, before the slave trade and since, have recorded cultural history and values through their stories."[11]

A "cultural continuity" also exists in the perpetuation of African values and customs in the Americas. "The cultural mores and values systems are passed down through the female members of the society, especially through and to the children."[12] Continuing this tradition, African American communities have attempted historically, through their women, to retrieve, re-gather and repair the often scattered and torn-apart roots of their African culture and reshape them in ways that are re-newing and re-viving for their people today. This is the wellspring out of which womanism pours forth. It reveals a critically different understanding of values and individual and communal responsibility.

Catholic womanist theologians seek to explore the intersection of race, class, gender, sexuality, and religion in an effort to reveal the role which the Christian religion, especially Roman

Catholicism, has played in affirming, exploiting, perpetuating, and upholding understandings of these social constructs which have served to provide not only a language but a pervasive, hegemonic ethos of subordination and oppression of women and persons of color. Grounded in the neo-platonic dualistic separation of the sacred and secular worlds, such an understanding has enabled the spread of a race-based hierarchical/patriarchal system which has supported the enslavement not just of other human beings but of other Christians, the dehumanization of women and persons of color and a stance that supports rather than challenges the oppression of so many.[13]

The challenge today is to look at these social constructs, including religion itself as it has come to be constituted in the United States, through eyes that have been opened by the recognition of the "other-createdness" from which they emerged. Dualistic systems allow for the emergence of an "either/or" understanding of life, knowledge, morality, and society. It enables the differentiation of human beings into "us and them," into "human and non-human," into those we recognize as friend and "others" by whom we feel threatened. It speaks a coldly sterile language of negativity, dualism, separation, subordination, and alienation.

I would like to offer three examples of how a womanist critical lens can take a story we have heard countless times and see it and its significance very differently. Let's look at the models of womanhood and femininity that have historically been such a significant part of our church's teachings on women. Mary, the mother of God, is contrasted eternally with either Eve, the alleged cause of humanity's fall into sin, or Mary Magdalene, the repentant sinner. Are these women so strikingly different from each other as they have been portrayed? First, a disclaimer: I am not a scripture scholar; I am simply attempting to recover the rest of the story, you might say. And when we read Genesis 2 and Luke with a critical womanist eye, we do see something very different.

Beginning appropriately with the text of Genesis and the second creation story, if we read carefully we find that nowhere in that story does it say that Eve committed a sin (her son, Cain, as the first murderer is the first sinner), nor is she cursed by God (only the serpent is), nor can it be said that she seduced or in any other way forced Adam to eat of the fruit of the tree in the garden's center. She is, ironically, the first person in the Bible to serve someone food (something women have been doing from then on). But she and Adam are expelled from the garden because they have acquired knowledge, that is, they have become thinking, aware human beings. It could be said that they have become fully human.

Yet many, if not most interpretations of this story attribute fault solely to Eve, the gateway, as she and all women have been called, of hell; a woman guilty, if of anything, only of seeking greater knowledge than was deemed good for her. From a womanist perspective, as the descendant of a people forbidden to learn how to read and write under pain of death but also, ironically, stigmatized as incapable of learning, being only at best "bright monkeys," Eve's story for black women is one not of sin but of courage and boldness. It is a story of persistence in the pursuit of knowledge, a persistence rewarded by an increase of pain (whether in childbirth or in struggling to learn under almost impossible conditions after a day of backbreaking labor) but it is a pain deemed worthy of repeating over and over again (as women do by bearing more than one child and the slaves and freed slaves did by persisting in their efforts to gain an education despite whippings, beatings, and being burned out of their homes and schools). The pain is overcome by the reward, greater knowledge, a goal historically deemed worthy of pursuit only by men, and white men at that.

Mary Magdalene has also been maligned down through the ages. For centuries venerated as the "Great Apostle" and the "Apostle to the Apostles" because of her unique role in being present at the resurrection as well as being commissioned by Jesus himself, the resurrected Christ, to spread the good news, the gospel, to others, she was unceremoniously demoted and commingled with other unnamed women in the New Testament, made over into a prostitute and repentant sinner. This is a stigma that remains to the present day despite the church's *sotto voce* reversal of that commingling in a footnote in the Roman Missal and John Paul II's acknowledgment of her, once again, as the Great Apostle. From a womanist perspective, the Magdalene speaks for and to countless unnamed black women, slave and free, who were condemned for their allegedly "sluttish" behavior, a lie put forth by the very men, Christian for the most part, who used their positions of power to rape them and even profit from the offspring produced as a result of that rape. Black women today must still live down the slander of being "jezebels," women with uncontrollable sexual appetites, as well as "sapphires" or "sistas with attitude" in the newest permutation of the same aspersion; that is, women who are willing to stand on their faith in themselves and their God in order to speak words of truth to their people, and anyone else that needs to hear, words that may seem harsh and at times unloving but that are spoken out of love and the effort to give life, as Mary Magdalene did.

Finally, there is the Virgin Mary. For two millennia we have been taught as women to revere and model ourselves after Mary, meek and mild, who humbly bowed her head and submitted unquestioningly to the will of God. Feminist theologian Elizabeth Johnson notes in her recent book about Mary[14] the words of author Mary Gordon:

> Mary was a stick to beat smart girls with. Her example was held up constantly: an example of silence, of sub-

ordination, of the pleasure of taking the back seat . . .
For women like me, it was necessary to reject the image
of Mary in order to hold onto the fragile hope of intellectual achievement, independence of identity, sexual
fulfillment.[15]

For Gordon and many like her, Johnson notes, "The Mar-
ian tradition is accused of distorting women's reality, of pro-
moting a restrictive ideal of human fulfillment, of constricting
women's social roles, of blocking their access to God's blessing
in the fullness of their lives. It has presided over the evil of sexism rather than challenged it."[16]

Once again, let us look at this story from a womanist perspective. Mary is, in today's understanding, still a child, barely
if at all into her teens. She is betrothed to a much older man, as
was the custom of the day. She is approached by the angel
Gabriel, who speaks to her words both mysterious and fright-
ening. But she does not simply accept what the angel has said
to her, she questions him, for she is understandably "troubled"
by his words. She is then told that, having found favor with
God, she will conceive and bear a son whom she will call Jesus.
Like many slave women, Mary is basically being told what her
life will be. Yet she again, probably to the angel's amazement,
questions him. As yet she has not been very meek or submissive; she wants to know *how* this is possible, *how* it will come
about. Gabriel's response is intended to resolve her fears and
confusion once and for all but, at the same time, to remind her
of the power of God. To further convince her, he tells her that
her cousin, Elizabeth, who Mary knows is not only barren but
also beyond her child-bearing years, has also conceived and is in
her sixth month of pregnancy. Only then does Mary agree to
the miracle about to unfold within her.

What is the significance of all of this? First, like Hagar, Mary
is being spoken to directly rather than through a man such as her

husband, father, uncle, and so forth. At the same time, she has not sought and does not seek permission from a man for her response, her "let it be done." Remember now, Mary, though betrothed, is still quite young and a virgin. But she knows the customs of her people and the consequence for being found pregnant prior to having been wed: it is harsh. She will be taken outside her village and stoned to death. She knows, therefore, that what she is being asked to agree to (and she *is* being asked as Gabriel, as we saw, has to convince her that all that he has said is possible) could cost her her life and would certainly derail her engagement to Joseph who, as we later read, does intend to break off the engagement once he discovers that she is pregnant.

We read the annunciation story in just a few minutes, but for Mary it surely took more time to make such a momentous decision. God does not force anyone; we, as humans, freely acquiesce to God's will, but we do so, not blindly, but knowing that saying a "yes" to God will irrevocably change our lives; there will certainly be consequences. And, indeed, the life of this young woman is changed forever, as is all of history. It can also be argued that, still unsure and even perhaps a bit disbelieving of all that has taken place, she quickly goes to visit Elizabeth to see for herself evidence of God's word. It is only when she encounters a heavily pregnant Elizabeth that she proclaims her faith in God in a magnificent song that stands to this day as a proclamation not of passivity or humility but of revolution, of a reversal of the status quo and the breaking forth of God's righteous justice into the world in the form of her son. Mary's song, like other songs by women in sacred scripture, is not a song of pious submission but one of righteous judgment and vindication for all who, like Mary and her son, are born poor and oppressed and unjustly victimized. She is prophesying the coming kin-dom of God, a time and place where those who are poor will receive God's bounty and those who are hungry will be fed while the rich and arrogant, those who are unjust, will be cast away. Is it any wonder that her son, Jesus, makes an almost identical prophetic statement in his first sermon?[17]

Mary, by saying yes to God, breaks open human history and subverts it, turning all of reality upside down, for she affirms and acknowledges that the miraculous work of God brought about through the Holy Spirit will result in a new reality for all of humanity. She stands, therefore, as a symbol of hope and courage for so many women, poor and invisible, who, by their actions throughout history, by their willingness to stand up and walk out on faith, like so many black Catholic women have done, bring about a new and better world for all of humanity. They and their children serve as catalysts for change in the world and for hope beyond it. Mary, therefore, is a sign of contradiction, and a model not of passivity or voicelessness, but a model for bold, daring, audacious, and courageous black Catholic women. She is a source of hope for young pregnant girls of today, children giving birth to children, for in her coming to voice through the intervention of her God, they can see the possibilities that exist in what would otherwise for so many seem a hopeless situation.

> Existentially, Mary's response carries with it a fundamental definition of personhood. Facing a critical choice, she sums herself up "in one of those great self-constituting decisions that give shape to a human life . . ." [T]his young woman's decision is not a passive, timid reaction but a free and autonomous act [that] encourages and endorses women's efforts to take responsibility for their own lives. The courage of her decision vis-à-vis the Holy One is at the same time an assent to the totality of herself.[18]

These three women, Eve, Mary of Magdala, and Mary, the Mother of God, are only a few of the women in sacred scripture who speak words of womanist wisdom and dare to become other than what they have been told they should be. Seen holistically, rather than dualistically; seen through the dark eyes of their black Catholic sisters who have borne the burden of rape, forced sterilization, children sold away or taken away by the state; loss of name, history, husband, family, all that makes up a human life, and denied their very humanity; yet these women told God it would be all right if he changed their names. For to be a woman named by God was to be a woman who changed the world around them. They are sisters in solidarity, rather than opposition, who speak words of black wisdom and live lives of black hope, courage, and faith in a world that saw them as nothing.

For Catholic womanist God-talk is rooted in the cycle of life and death rather than only death. It seeks always to bring forth life from that which was seen as lifeless, inhuman, and so often despised. It is the effort to constantly speak truth to life, knowing as poet Audre Lorde knew, that "we were not meant to survive."[19]

In so many ways, these women, along with Hagar, Deborah the Judge, Dinah the daughter of Jacob and so many other women, named and unnamed, down through the ages, were not meant to survive. At least, their stories as they would have had them told were not meant to survive as they would have had them survive, but were rewritten too often by others with a different agenda who knew nothing, and probably cared even less, of their pain and fears, their hopes and dreams. Theirs are stories that must be retrieved and retold "in memory of them" and countless other women whose spirits dwell among us still.

For Catholic womanist theologians, the ongoing challenge is to recover and reclaim these and so many other lives of black Catholic women, and men as well, whose lives cry out to be told. We must proclaim their lives boldly so that others may learn of and follow them. The task is not an easy one, for there are many other challenges that confront us as well. One of these, a critical one, is gaining the right to speak out in academia and the church from within our particular context, that is, specifically as black Catholic women. Patricia Hill Collins speaks of black women, especially those now in professional fields, as "outsiders-within."[20] Our positions as women with degrees at the master's or doctoral level, especially in institutions of higher learning, provide us with an "insider's" status, enabling us to participate to a certain degree in academic discourse and have an impact on others in those institutions. At the same time, however, because of our personal situations as black women, we are also "outsiders" whose views are not always welcomed and whose input is often trivialized. We find ourselves straddling two worlds, that of academia or other professions, and that of the black community with its often very different perspective. In order to truly belong to one or the other, it is assumed that we must give up our existence in the other, as they are not complementary. These assumptions, however, are cynically grounded too often in issues of power, control, and manipulation, yet again, of the black woman's reality.

> The exclusion of Black women's ideas from mainstream academic discourse and the curious placement of African American women intellectuals in feminist thinking, Black social and political theories, and in other important thought . . . has meant that U.S. Black women intellectuals have found themselves in outsider-within positions in many academic endeavors (Hull et al. 1982; Christian 1989). The assumptions on which full group membership are based—Whiteness for feminist thought, maleness for Black social and political thought, and the combination for mainstream scholarship—all negate Black women's realities. Prevented from becoming full insiders in any of these

areas of inquiry, Black women remain in outsider-within locations, individuals whose marginality provides a distinctive angle of vision on these intellectual and political entities.[21]

Attempting to survive in these often contradictory worlds is a constant and often enervating challenge that leaves you feeling as if you're being torn in several directions, required to make choices that have severe consequences not only for self-identity but also for the work that you are trying to do.

As womanist theologians, we seek to remove the masks that cover up the inherent illegitimacy of the existing forms of society and their use of language to exclude and restrict.[22] We do this by revealing other, more holistic, worldviews that serve to bring about unity rather than division, harmony rather than discord. As black women, we have come to realize that in order to authenticate ourselves and legitimate the work that we do, we must also remove the masks that have covered the many worlds in which we find ourselves. Only in so doing can we then present these masks to public view and develop a unified challenge to them and to those worlds with which they appear to conflict. The words, "appear to conflict" are used deliberately, for the reality is that they do not necessarily conflict but are made to appear so by those who are, in some way, threatened by them.

This means claiming the legitimacy of our being as black female professionals and working to develop a critical understanding of both past and present in order to participate in building a more holistic future, one in which persons like us will no longer be required to deny the totality of their being in order to "belong" but can embrace and be embraced for what they bring to intellectual and personal discourse in both the public and private arenas. In so doing, I, in company with my other sister womanists, seek to speak in ways that are understandable to these communities but with a preference toward the black and other marginalized communities, recognizing that I may, as a result, be accused of being too "popular," a term often used to denigrate the language of persons of color, women, and those lacking a string of letters after their name.

> My choice of language . . . typifies my efforts to theo-rize differently. A choice of language transcends mere selection of words—it is inherently a political choice . . . Writing . . . in a language that appears too "simple" might give grounds for criticism to those individuals who think that the complex ideas of social theory [and theology—DLH] must be abstract, difficult, and inac-cessible . . . Populist ideas become devalued exactly be-cause they are popular. This position reflects a growing disdain for anything deemed "public" and for the gen-eral public itself.[23]

Black women, as their community's bearers of culture, have, historically, been the forgers of new ways of being and speaking in the world. They recognize with Collins that, "[p]ri-vatizing and hoarding ideas upholds inequality. Sharing ideas through translation and teaching supports democracy."[24] It is our task today as Catholic womanists to speak life into the fu-ture, a future inclusive and representative of all. We do so by working to redefine what it means to be male and female in lan-guage that complements the actual experiences of those en-gaged in living out maleness and femaleness, in ways inclusive of both heterosexual and homosexual understandings. In our stories, songs, prayers, and God-talk (theologizing), black women speak life into being, not a stunted growth unable to flourish and condemned to premature death, nor one confined to dry, dusty tomes read and understood by only a privileged few, but a life that is fruitful and representative of a diversity created, not by human hands, but by divine ones.

Black women have, historically, worked to make community, a desire deeply rooted in their African ancestry and made even more important by their experiences in the United States.

> "Making community" means the processes of creating religious, educational, health-care, philanthropic, political, and familial institutions and professional organizations that enabled our people to survive. In the early eighteenth and nineteenth centuries, Black women "made Community" through the building and shaping of slave culture. Later the process of "making community" was repeated in post-emancipation agricultural areas and then in urban industrial societies ... It was through "making community" that Black women were able to redefine themselves, project sexual respectability, reshape morality, and define a new aesthetic.
>
> In sum, Black women came to subjecthood and acquired agency through the creation of community.[25]

Today we who name ourselves womanists do so, not in opposition but in creation, seeking to "make community" wherever we find ourselves. We define ourselves not over against but in solidarity with, affirming that new ways of self-definition must emerge, not as hand-me-downs or cast-offs of others' self-understanding but created out of the fabric of our own lives. In so doing we are creating a new language of liberation that is open to any and all that are willing to speak plainly without assuming their language will give them power and/or authority over another. As womanists, we see as our challenge the gathering of the myriad threads of the richly diverse black community and breathing into it renewed life which can serve as a model of life for our world. That model is centered on the co-createdness by God of all, regardless of efforts to separate by the arbitrary use of divisive language and beliefs which restrict rather than encourage the fullness of life and its possibilities. All who are oppressed share in solidarity with each other, a solidarity that should not be laid aside for individual desires or "battles." The struggle is communal, not individual, and can be won only if experiences are shared, stories are told, songs are sung, histories are reclaimed and restored, a new language emerges which speaks words of peace and unity, which unites, which recalls both the pain and the joy of our different heritages and leads us into a brand new day.

NOTES

1. Darlene Clark Hine, ed., *Encyclopedia of Black Women in America* (Bloomington, IN: Indiana University Press, 1994), 457.

2. Ibid., 459–60.

3. Delores Williams, *Sisters in the Wilderness: The Challenge of Womanist God-Talk,* (Maryknoll, NY: Orbis Books, 1993), 118.

4. Ibid.

5. Ibid., 119.

6. Bernice J. Reagan, "African Diaspora Women: The Making of Cultural Workers," in *Women in Africa and the African Diaspora*, ed. Rosalyn Terborg-Penn, Sharon Harley, and Andrea Benton Rushing, (Washington, DC: Howard University Press, 1987), 169.

7. Cyprian Davis, "God of Our Weary Years," in *Taking Down Our Harps: Black Catholics in the U.S.*, ed. Diana L. Hayes and Cyprian Davis, OSB (Maryknoll, NY: Orbis Books, 1999), 20.

8. Ibid., 30.

9. Cyprian Davis, *The History of Black Catholics in the United States* (New York: Crossroad, 1990), 115.

10. Diana L. Hayes, "And When We Speak," in *Taking Down Our Harps,* 106.

11. Gay Wilentz, *Binding Cultures: Black Women Writers in Africa and the Diaspora* (Bloomington: Indiana University Press, 1992), xii.

12. Ibid., v–xvi.

13. See Kelly Brown Douglas, *Sexuality and the Black Church: A Womanist Perspective* (Maryknoll, NY: Orbis Books, 1999), 2–29 and Hayes, "And When We Speak," 102–19.

14. Elizabeth A. Johnson, *Truly Our Sister: A Theology of Mary in the Communion of Saints* (New York: Continuum, 2004).

15. Ibid., 10–11.

16. Ibid., 11.

17. See Luke 4:16–30.

18. Johnson, *Truly Our Sister,* 257.

19. "A Litany for Survival" in *The Collected Poems of Audre Lorde* (New York: W. W. Norton, 1997), 255–56.

20. Patricia Hill Collins, *Black Feminist Thought: Knowledge, Consciousness and the Politics of Empowerment. Perspectives on Gender,* 2nd ed. (New York: Routledge, 2000), 11–13.

21. Ibid., 12.

22. Today, for example, we are confronted by an administration that claims to be acting on behalf of peace by instigating war, to be helping the poor and unemployed by providing tax cuts and write-offs for the rich, and to be helping students by requiring standardized tests for children as young as three and cutting back on loans and grants for higher education. The language is cast in words familiar and soothing, but the effect of the actions behind them is oppressive and life threatening to many.

23. Patricia Hill Collins, *Fighting Words: Black Women and the Search for Justice,* Contradictions of Modernity, vol. 7 (Minneapolis: University of Minnesota Press, 1998), xxi–xxii.

24. Ibid., xxiii.

25. Darlene Clark Hine, *Black Women and the Re-Construction of American History* (Bloomington: Indiana University Press, 1994), xxii.

10

Insistent Inclusion

Intersections of Race, Class, and Gender

Sometimes I feel Like a motherless child,
Sometimes I feel Like a motherless child,
Sometimes I feel like a motherless child,
A long way from home,
A long, long way from home
True believer, true believer
A long way from home

—Negro Spiritual

The words of this spiritual, sung in the dark hours before dawn and after dusk by many of my ancestors who were caught up in the holocaust that was slavery in the United States, continues to ring true for many African American women today. Born into a world and a society that speaks highly of women if they know and stay in their socially appointed places, hemmed in by oppressive religious values that claim to be based on the teachings of Jesus Christ, black women (and women as a whole) continue today to seek a "space" for themselves in which to be free.

First published in *Prophetic Witness: Catholic Women's Strategies for Reform*, ed. Coleen M. Griffith (New York: Crossroad, 2009) 159–67.

They are assaulted physically, spiritually, and emotionally on a daily basis by those whom they thought were friends and/or allies, the men in their lives as well as other women, and by the racism and sexism apparent in the societies in which they live. African American women too often are valued, not for their intelligence or their strength, but for their weight or lack thereof, the lightness or darkness of their skin, the size and prominence of their breasts and hips, and the texture of their hair. These are all superficial standards that seek to squeeze them into shapes and forms that inhibit and restrict. Never part of the myth of "True Womanhood," which placed white women on pedestals that were equally restrictive, African American women historically were never "good enough" and still today fail to reach the acceptable standards of contemporary society. Those who attempt to break out and stand on their own are labeled and demonized by church and society as "unfit mothers" and "unnatural women." Commenting on the social construction of African American women, Margaret Hunter wrote:

> The sexual and racial images of African American women as oversexed or whorish are also a direct reaction to the cult of white womanhood. Because black women were deliberately dehumanized, they were denied even a basic identity as women. When enslaved, they were forced to work alongside men in physically strenuous tasks, for long hours. They were not seen as pristine, dependent, passive, fragile, or as having any of the traits that defined white womanhood. Instead, African American women were used as workhorses who were forced to be always sexually available to white men. Black women were "de-feminized" because they occupied a gendered space for which there was no clear gender identity. They were wives and mothers, but they were also (unlike many white women) workers, inde-

pendent from men, and strong. This combination of traits left black women in a non-gendered space where they did not have access to the rights of men, nor did they share in the female protections of patriarchy.[1]

Why, in the twenty-first century, do African American women, as well as women of other races and ethnicities, still find themselves hemmed in by the constraints of race and gender constructed centuries ago, constructions that attempt to define and by so doing confine all of humanity, male and female? What is the origin of these constructions and why does their impact still reverberate down countless centuries to the present day? What role has religion, and Christianity in particular, played in the development and perpetuation of these definitional constraints?

This is an inquiry at the heart of womanist theology. Womanist theologians[2] seek to break the chains of societal "isms" that constrain and restrain women's rights to work in non-domestic roles, to live independent lives, and to speak for and about themselves in words of their own choosing. They seek to do this, not alone or just for themselves, but in order to build and rebuild the black community and all communities threatened with destruction due to an onslaught of values that counter those that historically kept us strong. Parochial values such as individualism, materialism, and consumerism divide rather than unite, tearing down rather than building up community. Womanist theologians seek to speak not for but in solidarity with their black sisters throughout the African diaspora, asking what it means to be a black woman in the twenty-first century, especially a Christian black woman.

Why must women, regardless of race or ethnicity, continue to fight for inclusion into worlds of which they have always been a significant, but overlooked part? Women make up more than half of the world's population yet still find it necessary to struggle to express themselves in meaningful ways without being constrained by the men in their lives. When they succeed in doing so, they are labeled unnatural and unfeminine.

In this essay, I seek to bring the voices and experiences of U.S. women of African descent to the forefront of the dialogue now taking place between the Christian churches and U.S. society. Black women's voices are ones that have not, historically, been included, despite the inroads that feminist thought has made in academia. Most black women are not feminists and those who are still struggle against the latent and often unconscious but egregious racism that persists in the feminist movement. Black women's lives have been defined by very different experiences, including the lingering impact of slavery and its virulent offspring, racism, sexism, and classism. They struggle to defend a faith that is theirs in Roman Catholic and Protestant Christian churches of which they have been a viable part since their beginnings in the United States. They are stretched painfully by the tension that persists between black women and men, a tension rooted in part in slavery but aggravated by the ways in which black men and women have consistently been pitted against one another in American society. Black women are torn by the pain of loved ones, the increase in women and children afflicted with HIV/AIDS, and the increasingly blatant and phobic heterosexism manifested in the leading churches of the black community by their ministers.

Black Women Today

Black women today find themselves in a familiar situation, caught between "a rock and a hard place" with seemingly all exits barred. This sadly is a situation they had to deal with in slavery when they were worked like oxen and bred like cattle. It is the situation they knew in the post-Reconstruction era, when they were slandered as women of loose morals who were perceived to be negative influences on their husbands and sons. And it is one experienced in the civil rights and black power movements, when women activists, with graduate degrees and years of experience, were relegated to roles behind the scenes as secretaries and "comfort" women.

Delores Williams speaks of this experience in her discussion of the story of Hagar, found in the book of Genesis. Hagar, like many slave women, was forced to have sexual intercourse with her master, and then she was beaten by her mistress when she successfully became pregnant. Yet when she ran away, she was sent back into slavery by God, only to be finally expelled from her community with her son, Ishmael, with little hope of survival. Yet she was given the same promise by God that God gave to Abram, that her descendants would be many, her line would not run dry.

The story of Hagar, as Williams notes, provides insight into why womanists emphasize survival over the liberation invoked by most black male theologians. While womanists acknowledge that liberation is important and that those enslaved must act with God's assistance to free themselves, it does not prove enough. What good is freedom if it only leads to the death of oneself and one's family as a result of homelessness, disease, and eventual starvation? Liberation is viable only after one has learned to survive and to provide for oneself and those around oneself a quality of life that ensures the survival of that liberation. Williams comments on this, referencing Hagar:

> Like African American people, Hagar and her child are alone without resources for survival. Hagar must try to make a living in the wide, wide world for herself and her child. This was also the task of many African American women and the entire community of Black people freed when emancipation came.[3]

Williams continues:

> The post-bellum notion of wilderness (with Hagar and child as its content) emphasized black women's and the black community's negative experience of poverty and social displacement... This post-bellum African American symbolic sense of wilderness, with Hagar at its center, makes the female figure symbolic of the entire black community's history of brutalization during slavery; of fierce survival struggle and servitude after liberation; of children being cheated out of their inheritance by oppressors; of threat to the life and well-being of the family; of the continuing search for a positive, productive quality of life for women and men under God's care.[4]

This was the situation in which blacks found themselves at the end of the Civil War and after the end of the short-lived period of hope called Reconstruction. Like Hagar, they found it necessary to return, many of them, to the very plantations on which they had been enslaved and to accept a life of subservience known as sharecropping. They did this while working diligently and also furtively to gain the skills which would enable them or their children or their children's children to escape and forge new lives out of the wilderness of Jim Crow's *de jure* form of slavery that persisted well beyond the 1960s and was not limited to only the Southern states as most assume.

It is from within this context, as a descendant of slaves, sharecroppers, farmers, and domestics that I speak as a womanist theologian today. I am a first-generation college educated African American woman; a convert in my adulthood from the historically black African Methodist Episcopal Zion (AMEZion) church to the Roman Catholic Church, a predominantly white church as it is seen but one that both historically and today is made up predominantly of persons of color. An attorney, and now a theologian, I have spent most of my life grappling with issues that assault the very core of my being, not just the usual question of "who am I?" but, as others have repeatedly asked, "what am I?" Having been born into working class poverty yet now, because of my educational achievements and professional status, a part of the upper middle class, my journey has exposed me to class, race, and gender discrimination. I have fought to achieve my goals of higher education while having to constantly defend my presence and existence as a black woman of intelligence. Patricia Hill Collins describes my experience and that of other black women intellectuals very well:

> The exclusion of Black women's ideas from mainstream academic discourse and the curious placement of African American women intellectuals in both feminist and Black social and political thought has meant that Black women intellectuals have remained outsiders within in all three communities. The assumptions on which full group membership are based . . . whiteness for feminist thought, maleness for Black social and political thought, and the combination for mainstream scholarship . . . all negate a Black female reality. Prevented from becoming full insiders in any of these areas of inquiry, Black women remain outsiders within, individuals whose marginality provides a distinctive angle of vision on the theories put forth by such intellectual communities.[5]

Just as most people are born into a religion, that of their parents or grandparents usually, and remain there all of their lives, we are born into our skins and our sexualities. No one decides in the womb what race or sex they will be; it is an act of God and the random mixing of our parents' genetic contributions. These are most certainly not a choice.

But church and society have established an elaborate set of attributes and responsibilities based allegedly on scientific "facts" that serve to designate supposed proper roles for men and women, blacks and whites. Similar "facts" with scripture used to support them were used to support and condone the infamy and horror of slavery in the Americas. Have we learned nothing from that experience? It seems not.

The Social Construction of Persons

The world we live in today is increasingly complex while, at the same time, incredibly diverse. People from cultures with very different traditions find themselves praying and celebrating the Eucharist together, sharing histories and stories in classrooms, and working together in the business world. The shifting demographics of the United States are reflected in our daily encounters and force us to recognize changes needed and changes that will come, welcomed or unwelcomed. We no longer live in a naive world leading simple lives, if ever we did. It is incumbent upon all of us, and not just the poor, or immigrants, or persons of color, but white men, who still occupy most of the positions of leadership in U.S. society and its churches, and white women as well, who share in the rewards of white privilege, to begin to acknowledge the ways in which our lives have been socially constructed and to work to eliminate the harmful impact of these constructions.

All of us, and not just a few, are affected when persons of intellectual ability are restricted in the quality of education they receive or in their access to higher education, because of race, gender, class, or sexual orientation. Those in positions of leadership and power (often the kind of power passed on from father to son and friend to friend) have defined how these terms, race, class, and gender are to be lived. Upon these human constructions towering edifices have been built that hem in and constrain rather than allow persons to explore and expand the myriad possibilities of their being. The results have been disastrous for too many.

Ironically, it is often people who have experienced oppression or marginalization and who, having been liberated and having achieved positions of authority, turn around and restrict, restrain or "punish" others of whom they do not approve. We have seen this happen over and over in history yet still refuse to learn from it. The conquered vanquish their conquerors and then become as oppressive as those who oppressed them. A rare and refreshing shift from this pattern has been South Africa, which has fought and struggled to heal the wounds of its painful apartheid past without making martyrs of those who for so long a time martyred them.

The Catholic Church has seemingly not learned the lessons of its two-thousand-year-long history. Although the Vatican categorically denounced slavery in any and all forms in 1965, a brief forty-plus years ago, the church still persists in upholding degrading and exclusive structures that the rest of the world has long forgotten. As a divine and human institution, the church should attempt to learn from the history which is very much its own and repent of its sins. As Pope John made clear at the opening of the Second Vatican Council, the church is not perfect but is seeking perfection. It will thrive in its fullest form as the people of God, which means all of the faithful and not just a few with particular titles who are ordained. We are all called to be priests in the fullest understanding of ministry, in and through our baptism, and that calling demands respect for the basic dignity of all human beings as created in the image and likeness of God, regardless of race, class, sexuality, or sexual orientation. People are to be respected and seen as an aspect of

God's grace. Although Pope John Paul II apologized for the devastation of slavery and the church's role in its implementation in Africa and the Americas in the year 2000, the impact of that apology has been minimal in the worldwide church.

On Whiteness and Blackness

Whiteness, blackness, or any aspect of color used to divide and separate can be traced back to the laws that the United States established in the seventeenth century as a means of designating who was intended (allegedly) by God to be free (whites) and to be a slave (blacks). The arbitrariness of this designation can be seen in myriad laws that have followed in the wake of the initial designation, laws that were required to decide who could claim "whiteness" with all of the benefits of white privilege and who could not. The understanding of "whiteness" has shifted many times. It has included and excluded Native Americans, Asians, Arabs, and Latinos/as as well as many ethnic groups today considered white but who were not so designated when they first migrated to this country, such as Italians, Irish, and Jews. Results of court decisions regarding "whiteness" have led to suicides, to internments, and to various forms of apartheid that continue to haunt us to the present day. The reasoning behind these shifts in designation is deeply rooted in the proof-texting of scripture, though the main undergirding factor has been economic: how to obtain the greatest number of laborers at the least expense.

Whiteness historically and to a great extent today exists only in the presence of blackness, a reality that has bound up the United States in a binary construct that continues to ignore the presence of others who are neither black nor white. Patricia Hill Collins comments:

> Based on the struggle for power in society, racial categories are manipulated and transformed to guarantee

one segment of the population, whites, the largest portion of resources. Consequently the boundaries of the races are always changing and who is included in which category changes with politics, economics, and the historical moment.[6]

Critical consciousness of how racial categories function is sorely needed in our time.

The Intersection of Race, Class, and Gender in the Aftermath of Hurricane Katrina

Recently we witnessed in the United States a horrific example of the ways in which race, class, and gender can intersect to the detriment of thousands. I am referring to the chaos that ensued on the Gulf Coast and the city of New Orleans as a result of Hurricanes Katrina and Rita. These hurricanes revealed the racism that still persists in the United States, coupled with poverty, and they exposed the feminization of poverty. The face of Katrina's devastation that was flashed around the world on television, newspapers, computer screens, and journal covers was that of a distraught, half-drowned black woman clutching one or more children to her breast. This is the face of America in the twenty-first century. As Loretta Ross notes:

> Poverty in America is not only racialized but it is also gendered. The aftermath of Katrina must be examined through a gender lens that identifies the myriad of violations experienced by women. A disaster like Katrina is a violation against the entire community, but when threats to women's lives are not recognized, and steps are not taken to ensure that they are, women become doubly victimized—by the disaster and by the response to it.[7]

The hurricane and the subsequent flooding highlighted the particular vulnerability of women, children, the elderly, and the disabled, underscoring the complex intersections of race, class, gender, ability, and life expectancy. Ross continues: "Many people could not escape not only because of poverty, but because they were not physically able to punch through rooftops, perch on top of buildings, or climb trees to survive"[8]

Incredibly, the media and government at every level sought to place blame on those who died for making incorrect or poor choices. The truth, however, is that a majority of those who died did so in their attics and living rooms, or found themselves abandoned in the Superdome without food, water, and medicines or dumped and left stranded on Interstate 10 in blazing heat for more than four days, because they *had no choice*. They were left to the mercy of others who should have taken the responsibility to ensure their safety but who, like Pontius Pilate (Mt 27:15–26), washed their hands of that responsibility and thereby washed away thousands, claiming that they had to use their own initiative to escape the rising waters. Some religious commentators placed blame on single black mothers for their plight, asserting that if they had married the father of their children, they would have been at a higher economic status and would therefore not have suffered as they did. Such comments obviously ignore the fact that many of those who were married and with children in New Orleans lived below the poverty line and had no access to a car or any other form of private transportation.

How did this come about? Quite simply because those in positions of leadership, who speak all of the right words—"love thy neighbor, care for the widow and the orphan, ensure the health and prosperity of all"—do not live the message they preach. What we, in fact, have seen take place in the United States is the abandonment of the "least among us," the removal of any and all "safety nets," and the denial of basic human rights owed to all human beings because of their creation by God.

And What About the Church?

The situation in the Catholic Church is similar, albeit not as blatant. Women are denied positions of leadership based on "man"-made laws; gay priests and seminarians are being forced to deny their vocations because of the refusal to recognize that pedophilia and homosexuality have nothing in common and that celibacy is viable for them just as for heterosexuals. The church has become a bully towards those who are "the least among us" while claiming to protect them. The long Catholic social justice tradition shows how the church has spoken and at times acted with a "preferential option for the poor" but we also have seen how we have stomped on the rights and human-ity of those who dare to speak in ways that, while still clearly a part of our tradition, don't fit the narrow and often untheolog-ical thinking of those in positions of authority. Rather than opening up to dialogue, some in positions of power within the institutional church find it simpler to condemn, silence, with-draw privileges, close down, shut down, deny, and/or excom-municate. Why does the church, which is of God, fear God's word coming from the mouths of others who, like the children Jesus blessed, speak a wisdom grounded in generations of a deep and abiding faith? The church denies that it changes, but anyone with eyes to see and ears to hear can see that it does and has repeatedly over the course of two thousand years. Some of these changes, for the most part, have been very beneficial, but today many shifts are simply reactionary responses to the "signs of the times," not in the least what the church fathers (and mothers, although not allowed to speak in public) had in mind when writing the challenging words of *Gaudium et Spes*.

A Spiritual Practice of Insistent Inclusion

It is the faith-filled who are the people of God and who are speaking out in the church today. They are seeking to remind it of its humble origins and calling it to return to its roots in Africa and the Middle East, albeit not the Africa of today, which is tied up in contradiction and restriction as a result of colonialism and its failures, nor the Middle East of today, caught up in a life-and-death struggle between peoples who claim to believe in and follow the same God. A return is called for and it is a return to the early church, which was a persecuted church, before it became entangled in the imperial webs of Rome and Christendom. In other words, it was a church of the poor, of slaves, and of women.

It is to this church and the man Jesus that my ancestors turned when they found themselves "way down yonder" by themselves, unable to hear anybody pray. Their belief was in a wonder-working God who helped them to get over the obstacles and traps that others set before them. Their God was a stern and righteous God, yes, but also a God of love and justice who sought to make a way out of no way for those in dire need. Jesus was to them a companion and a friend, a helpless infant and a lover, a brother and a sister, a mother and a father, a liberator who came "to set the captives free" and not entangle them in so many rules and restrictions that God Godself was lost sight of.

"Neither Jew nor Greek, neither slave nor free, neither male nor female, we are all one in Christ Jesus" (Galatians 3:26–28). This is the vision of church that we should be seeking to fulfill in our world today. Women and men are different biologically, yes, but those biological differences do not make one superior to the other in any way. We each have been given particular gifts and charisms, sprinkled by God across all of humanity regardless of gender, race, class, or sexual orientation: to preach, to proclaim, to exhort, to teach, to comfort, and to heal. These are found in men and women, gay and straight, of every race and nation, speaking every tongue as those who followed Jesus, including his mother Mary, Mary of Magdala known as the Great Apostle, and many other women and men, named and unnamed. Jesus gave his mandate to proclaim the good news, the gospel message of his resurrection, to a woman, Mary of Magdala, calumnied much too long by a church apparently fearful of the powers of women.

Today we must teach, preach, pray, and proclaim that good news far and wide while recognizing the equal legitimacy of its proclamation in every language and by every people. No one nation or ethnic group has proprietary rights to Jesus, except perhaps the Jews of whom he was born. All the rest of us gentiles came to him late and had to learn of his ways.

As I understand the Christian message, we are sent to preach the gospel to the people as they are rather than to force them to become something or someone else. Insistent inclusion means continuing to fight for the rights of all, both in the church and in society. All are to be welcome, regardless of race, class, gender, sexual orientation, physical or mental ability, culture or ethnicity, or native tongue. Jesus came to the people as they were. Should not the church and our societies, allegedly based on the vision of Jesus Christ, do the same?

We betray our calling as the people of God who make up this pilgrim church when we seek to restrict its membership or inhibit the actions and thoughts of its members in ways that Jesus never demanded. We must recognize the limitation of the human-made laws that restrict us and, as Martin Luther King Jr. affirmed, acknowledge God's natural law while recognizing our own subjectivity. The church is not just European; it is and has always been African and Asian, and it is increasingly South and Central American, Eastern European, and of course North American.

Where would Christianity be without the women who led its first humble home churches and passed down the teachings to the children? Where would it be without the faithful poor, of every race and ethnicity, who believed God would help them in their direst straits, even if only by listening to their cries? Where would it be without the many that maintained and sustained it, who suffered martyrdom for their faith, who passed it on despite all that was done to them? Where would our church be? Perhaps where it is today, floundering in a morass of shame and denial with the spectacle of the hierarchy scandalizing the faithful rather than allegedly heretical theologians doing so. The motherless children are reclaiming their church and insisting that their presence and contributions be not just welcomed and affirmed but also included in the history, traditions and teachings of the Church today.

NOTES

1. Margaret L. Hunter, *Race, Gender, and the Politics of Skin Tone* (New York: Routledge, 2005), 31.

2. "Womanist" is a reference to the distinctive theology of African American women.

3. Delores Williams, *Sisters in the Wilderness: The Challenge of Womanist God-Talk* (Maryknoll, NY: Orbis Books, 1995), 118.

4. Ibid.

5. Patricia Hill Collins, *Black Feminist Thought: Knowledge, Consciousness, and the Politics of Empowerment,* 2nd ed. (New York: Routledge, 2000), 12; also see fuller discussion in pp. 11–13.

6. Ibid., 9.

7. Loretta Ross, "A Feminist Perspective on Katrina," www.zmag.org (October 10, 2005).

8. Ibid.

Further Reading on Womanist Spirituality

Bridges, Flora Wilson. *Resurrection Song: African American Spirituality*. Maryknoll, NY: Orbis Books, 2001.

Brown, Teresa Fry. *God Don't Like Ugly: African American Women Handing on Spiritual Values*. Nashville, TN: Abingdon Press, 2003.

————. *Can a Sister Get a Little Help?: Encouragement for Black Women in Ministry*. Cleveland. OH: The Pilgrim Press, 2008.

Collins, Bettye. *Jesus, Jobs and Justice: African American Women and Religion*. New York: Knopf, 2010.

Cook, Suzan. *Sister to Sister: Devotions to and From African American Women*. Valley Forge, PA: Judson Press, 1995.

Gayles, Gloria Wade. *My Soul Is a Witness*. Boston, MA: Beacon Press, 2002.

Gilkes, Cheryl. *If It Wasn't for the Women: Black Women's Experience and Womanist Culture in Church and Community*. Maryknoll, NY: Orbis Books, 2000.

Hayes, Diana L. *Hagar's Daughters: Womanist Ways of Being in the World*. Mahwah, NJ: Paulist Press, 1995.

————. *Trouble Don't Last Always: Soul Prayers*. Collegeville, MN: Liturgical Press, 1995.

————. *Were You There? Stations of the Cross*. Maryknoll, NY: Orbis Books, 1999.

————. *Forged in a Fiery Furnace: African American Spirituality*. Maryknoll, NY: Orbis Books, 2012.

Higginbotham, Evelyn Brooks. *Righteous Discontent: The Women's Movement in the Black Baptist Church*. Cambridge, MA: Harvard University Press, 1994.

Hull, Akasha Gloria. *Soul Talk: New Spirituality of African American Women*. Rochester, VT: Inner Traditions, 2001.

Mitchem, Stephanie. *Introducing Womanist Theology*. Maryknoll, NY: Orbis Books, 2002.

Riggs, Marcia. *Plenty Good Room: Women against Male Power in the Black Church*. Eugene, OR: Wipf and Stock, 2008.

Ryan, Judylyn. *Spirituality as Ideology in Black Women's Film and Literature*. Charlottesville, VA: University of Virginia, 2005.

Terrell, JoAnne. *Power in the Blood*. Maryknoll, NY: Orbis Books, 1998.

Townes, Emilie. *A Troubling in My Soul: Womanist Perspectives on Evil and Suffering*. Maryknoll, NY: Orbis Books, 1993.

———. *Womanist Justice, Womanist Hope* America Academy of Religion Series No. 79. Oxford, UK: Oxford University Press, 1993.

———. *In a Blaze of Glory: Womanist Spirituality as Social Witness*. Nashville, TN: Abingdon Press, 1995.

———. *Embracing the Spirit: Womanist Perspectives on Hope, Salvation and Transformation*. Maryknoll, NY: Orbis Books, 1997.

———. *Breaking the Fine Rain of Death: African American Health Issues and a Womanist Ethic of Care*. Eugene, OR: Wipf and Stock, 2002.

Townes, Emilie, with Stephanie Mitchem. *Faith, Health and Healing in African American Life*. Santa Barbara, CA: Praeger, 2008.

Walker, Alice. *In Search of Our Mother's Garden: Womanist Prose*. New York: Harcourt Brace Jovanovich, 1983.

Weems, Renita. *Just a Sister Away: A Womanist Vision of Women's Relationships in the Bible*. Publishing/Editing Network, 1991.

———. *I Asked for Intimacy: Stories of Blessings, Betrayals and Birthings*. Publishing/Editing Network, 1993.

———. *Listening for God: A Ministers Journey Through Silence and Doubt*. NY: Touchstone (Simon and Shuster), 2000.

———. *Showing Mary: How Women Can Share Prayers*. W. Bloomfield, MI: Walk Worthy Press, 2002.

———. *What Matters Most: Ten Lessons in Living Passionately*. W. Bloomfield, MI: Walk Worthy Press, 2004.

———. *Praise Is What We Do: Worshipping God from Head to Feet*. Nashville, TN: Abingdon, 2010.